William Winter

Gray days and gold in England and Scotland

William Winter

Gray days and gold in England and Scotland

ISBN/EAN: 9783743313729

Manufactured in Europe, USA, Canada, Australia, Japa

Cover: Foto ©ninafisch / pixelio.de

Manufactured and distributed by brebook publishing software (www.brebook.com)

William Winter

Gray days and gold in England and Scotland

GRAY DAYS AND GOLD

GRAY DAYS AND GOLD

IN ENGLAND AND SCOTLAND

BY

WILLIAM WINTER

NEW EDITION

NEW YORK
MACMILLAN AND COMPANY
AND LONDON
1893

COPYRIGHT, 1892,
BY MACMILLAN AND CO.

Set up and electrotyped June, 1892.
Reprinted November, 1892; January, 1893.

Norwood Press:
J. S. Cushing & Co. — Berwick & Smith.
Boston, Mass., U.S.A.

TO

Augustin Daly

REMEMBERING A FRIENDSHIP

OF MANY YEARS

I DEDICATE THIS BOOK

"*Est animus tibi*
Rerumque prudens, et secundis
Temporibus dubiisque rectus"

PREFACE.

This book, *a companion to* "Shakespeare's England," *relates* to the *gray days of an American wanderer in the British islands, and to the gold of thought and fancy that can be found there.* In "Shakespeare's England" *an attempt was made to depict, in an unconventional* manner, *those lovely scenes that* are *intertwined with* the *name and the* memory *of Shakespeare,* and *also to reflect* the *spirit of* that *English scenery in general which, to* an *imaginative mind, must always be venerable* with historic *antiquity and tenderly hallowed with poetic and romantic association.* The *present book continues the same treatment of kindred themes, referring not only* to *the* land *of Shakespeare but to the land of Burns* and

Scott. After so much had been done, and superbly done, by Washington Irving and by other authors, to celebrate the beauties of our ancestral home, it was perhaps an act of presumption on the part of the present writer to touch those subjects. He can only plead, in extenuation of his boldness, an irresistible impulse of reverence and affection for them. His presentment of them can give no offence, and perhaps it may be found sufficiently sympathetic and diversified to awaken and sustain at least a momentary interest in the minds of those readers who love to muse and dream over the relics of a storied past. If by happy fortune it should do more than that, — if it should help to impress his countrymen, so many of whom annually travel in Great Britain, with the superlative importance of adorning the physical aspect and of refining the material civilisation of America by a reproduction within its borders of whatever is valuable in the long experience and whatever is noble and beautiful in the domestic and religious spirit of the British islands, — his labour will not have been in vain. The supreme need of this age in America is a practical conviction that progress does not consist in material prosperity but in spiritual advancement. Utility has long been exclusively worshipped. The welfare of the future lies in the worship of beauty. To that worship these pages are devoted, with all that it implies of sympathy with the higher instincts and faith in the divine destiny of the human race.

Many of the sketches here assembled were originally printed in the New York Tribune, with which journal their author has been continuously associated as a contributor since 1865. They have been revised for publication in this form. Most of the paper on Sir Walter Scott first appeared in Harper's Weekly, for which periodical also the author has written many things. The paper on the Wordsworth country was contributed to the New York Mirror. The alluring field of Scottish antiquity and romance, which the

*author has ventured but slightly to touch,
may perhaps be explored hereafter, for treasures
of contemplation that earlier seekers
have left ungathered. The fact is recorded
that an important recent book called Shakespeare's
True Life, written by James Walter,
incorporates into its text, without credit,
several passages of original description and
reflection taken from the present writer's
sketches of the Shakespeare country, and also
quotes, as his work, an elaborate narrative
of a nocturnal visit to Anne Hathaway's
cottage, which he never wrote and never
claimed to have written. This statement is
made as a safeguard against future injustice.*

W. W.

1892.

CONTENTS.

CHAP.		PAGE
I.	CLASSIC SHRINES	15
II.	HAUNTED GLENS AND HOUSES	27
III.	OLD YORK	40
IV.	THE HAUNTS OF MOORE	55
V.	BEAUTIFUL BATH	72
VI.	THE LAND OF WORDSWORTH	80
VII.	SHAKESPEARE RELICS AT WORCESTER	98
VIII.	BYRON AND HUCKNALL-TORKARD	109
IX.	HISTORIC NOOKS AND CORNERS	133
X.	SHAKESPEARE'S TOWN	142
XI.	UP AND DOWN THE AVON	167
XII.	RAMBLES IN ARDEN	175

CONTENTS.

CHAP.		PAGE
XIII.	THE STRATFORD FOUNTAIN	183
XIV.	BOSWORTH FIELD	195
XV.	THE HOME OF DR. JOHNSON	209
XVI.	FROM LONDON TO EDINBURGH	224
XVII.	INTO THE HIGHLANDS	233
XVIII.	HIGHLAND BEAUTIES	241
XIX.	THE HEART OF SCOTLAND	253
XX.	SIR WALTER SCOTT	269
XXI.	ELEGIAC MEMORIALS	296
XXII.	SCOTTISH PICTURES	308
XXIII.	IMPERIAL RUINS	315
XXIV.	THE LAND OF MARMION	324

"*Whatever withdraws us from the power of our senses, whatever makes the past, the distant, or the future predominate over the present, advances us in the dignity of thinking beings.* . . . *All travel has its advantages. If the passenger visits better countries he may learn to improve his own, and if fortune carries him to worse he may learn to enjoy it.*"—DR. JOHNSON.

"*There is given,
Unto the things of earth which Time hath bent,
A spirit's feeling; and where he hath leant
His hand, but broke his scythe, there is a power
And magic in the ruined battlement,
For which the palace of the present hour
Must yield its pomp, and wait till ages are its
   dower.*"

BYRON.

GRAY DAYS AND GOLD.

I.

CLASSIC SHRINES.

LONDON, JUNE 29, 1888. — The poet Emerson's injunction, "Set not thy foot on graves," is wise and right; and being in merry England in the month of June it certainly is your own fault if you do not fulfil the rest of the philosophical commandment and "Hear what wine and roses say." Yet the history of England is largely written in her ancient churches and crumbling ruins, and the pilgrim to historic and literary shrines in this country will find it difficult to avoid setting his foot on graves. It is possible here, as elsewhere, to live entirely in the present; but to certain temperaments and in certain moods the temptation is irresistible to live mostly in the past. I write these words in a house that was once occupied by Nell Gwynn, and as I glance into the garden I see a venerable acacia that was planted by her own fair hands, in the far-off time of the Merry Monarch. Within a few days I have stood in the dungeon of Guy Fawkes, in the Tower, and sat at luncheon in a manor-house of Warwickshire wherein were once convened the conspirators of the Gunpowder Plot. The newspapers of this morning announce that a monument will be dedicated on July 19 to commemorate the defeat of the Spanish Armada, three hundred years ago. Surely it is not unnatural that some of us should live in the past and often should find ourselves musing over its legacies.

One of the most sacred spots in England is the churchyard of Stoke-Pogis. I revisited that place on June 13 and once again rambled and meditated in that hallowed haunt. Not many months ago it seemed likely that Stoke Park would pass into the possession of a sporting ring and be turned into a race-course and kennel. A track had already been laid there. Fate was kind, however, and averted the final disaster. Only a few changes are to be noted in that part of the park which to the reverent pilgrim must always be dear. The churchyard has been extended in front, and a solid wall of flint, pierced by an oak porch, richly carved, has replaced the plain fence, with its simple turnstile, that formerly enclosed that rural cemetery. The additional land was given by the new proprietor of Stoke Park, who wished that his own tomb might be made in it; and this has been built beneath a large tree not far from the entrance. The avenue from the gate to the church has been widened, and it is now fringed with thin lines of twisted stone; and where once stood only two or three rose-trees there are now sixty-two — set in lines on either side of the path. But the older part of the graveyard remains unchanged. The yew-trees cast their dense shade, as of old. The quaint porch of the sacred building has not suffered under the hand of restoration. The ancient wooden memorials of the dead continue to moulder above their ashes. And still the abundant ivy gleams and trembles in the sunshine and in the summer wind that plays so sweetly over the spired tower and dusky walls of this lovely temple —

"All green and wildly fresh without,
But worn and gray beneath."

It would still be a lovely church, even if it were not associated with the immortal Elegy. I stood for a long time beside the tomb of the noble and tender poet and looked with deep emotion on the surrounding scene of pensive, dream-like beauty — the great elms, so dense of foliage, so stately and graceful; the fields of deep, waving grass, golden with buttercups and white with daisies; the many unmarked mounds; the many mouldering tombstones; the rooks sailing and cawing around the tree-tops; and over all the blue sky flecked with floating fleece. Within the church nothing has been changed. The memorial window to Gray, for which contributions have been taken during several years, has not yet been placed. As I cast a farewell look at Gray's tomb, on turning to leave the churchyard, it rejoiced my heart to see that two American ladies, who had then just come in, were placing fresh flowers over the poet's dust. He has been buried more than a hundred years — but his memory is as bright and green as the ivy on the tower within whose shadow he sleeps, and as fragrant as the roses that bloom at its base. Many Americans visit Stoke-Pogis churchyard, and surely no visitor to the old world, who knows how to value what is best in its treasures, will omit that act of reverence. The journey is easy. A brief run by railway from Paddington takes you to Slough, which is near to Windsor, and thence it is a charming drive, or a still more charming walk, mostly through green, embowered lanes, to the "ivy-mantled tower," the "yew-trees' shade," and the simple tomb of Gray. What a gap there would be in the poetry of our language if the *Elegy in a Country Churchyard* were absent from it! By that sublime and tender reverie upon the most important of all subjects that can engage the attention of the human mind Thomas Gray became one of the chief benefactors of his race. Those lines have been murmured by the lips of sorrowing affection beside many a shrine of buried love and hope, in many a churchyard all round the world. The sick have remembered them with comfort. The great soldier, going into battle, has said them for his solace and cheer. The dying statesman, closing his weary eyes upon this empty world, has spoken them with his last faltering accents, and fallen asleep with their heavenly music in his heart. Well may we pause and ponder at the grave of that divine poet! Every noble mind is made nobler, every good heart is made better, for the experience of such a pilgrimage. In such places as these pride is rebuked, vanity is dispelled, and the revolt of the passionate human heart is humbled into meekness and submission.

There is a place kindred with Stoke-Pogis churchyard, a place destined to become, after a few years, as famous and as dear to the heart of the reverent pilgrim in the footsteps of genius and pure renown. On Sunday afternoon (June 17) I sat for a long time beside the grave of Matthew Arnold. It is in a little churchyard at Laleham in Surrey, where he was born. The day was chill, sombre, and, except for an occasional low twitter of birds and the melancholy cawing of distant rooks, soundless and sadly calm. So dark a sky might mean November rather than June; but it fitted well with the scene and with the pensive thoughts and feelings of the hour. Laleham is a village on the south bank of the Thames, about thirty miles from London and nearly midway between Staines and Chertsey. It consists of a few devious lanes and a cluster of houses, shaded with large trees and everywhere made beautiful with flowers, and it is one of those fortunate and happy places to which access cannot be obtained by railway. There is a great house in the centre of it, secluded in a walled garden, fronting the square immediately opposite to the village church. The rest of the houses are mostly cottages made of red brick and roofed with red tiles. Ivy flourishes, and many of the cottages are overrun with climbing roses. Roman relics are found in the neighbourhood — a camp near the ford, and other indications of the military activity of Cæsar. The church, All Saints', is of great antiquity. It has been in part restored, but its venerable aspect is not impaired. The large low tower is of brick, and this and the church walls are thickly covered with glistening ivy. A double-peaked roof of red tiles, sunken here and there, contributes to the picturesque beauty of this building, and its charm is further heightened by the contiguity of trees, in which the old church seems to nestle. Within there are low, massive pillars and plain, symmetrical arches — the remains of Norman architecture. Great rafters of dark oak augment in this quaint structure the air of solidity and of an age at once venerable and romantic, while a bold, spirited, beautiful painting of Christ and Peter upon the sea imparts to it an additional sentiment of sanctity and solemn pomp. That remarkable work is by George Henry Harlow, and it is placed back of the altar, where once there would have been, in the Gothic days, a stained window. The explorer does not often come upon such a gem of a church even in England — so rich in remains of the old Catholic zeal and devotion; remains now mostly converted to the use of Protestant worship.

The churchyard of All Saints' is worthy of the church — a little enclosure, irregular in shape, surface, shrubbery, and tombstones, bordered on two sides by the village square and on one by a farmyard, and shaded by many trees, some of them yews, and some of great size. Almost every house that is visible near by is bowered with trees and adorned with flowers. No person was anywhere to be seen, and it was only after inquiry at various dwellings that the sexton's abode could be discovered and access to the church obtained. The poet's grave is not within the church, but in a secluded spot at the side of it, a little removed from the highway, and screened from immediate view by an ancient dusky yew-tree. I readily found it, perceiving a large wreath of roses and a bunch of white flowers that were lying upon it,—recent offerings of tender remembrance and sorrowing love, but already beginning to wither. A small square of turf, bordered with white marble, covers the tomb of the poet and of three of his children.[1] At the head are three crosses of white marble, alike in shape and equal in size, except that the first is set upon a pedestal a little lower than those of the others. On the first cross is written: "Basil Francis Arnold, youngest child of Matthew and Frances Lucy Arnold. Born August 19, 1866. Died January 4, 1868. Suffer little children to come unto me." On the second: "Thomas Arnold, eldest child of Matthew and Frances Lucy Arnold. Born July 6, 1852. Died November 23, 1868. Awake, thou, Lute and Harp! I will awake right early." On the third: "Trevener William Arnold, second child of Matthew and Fran-

[1] Since these words were written a plain headstone of white marble has been placed on this spot bearing the following inscription:—

"Matthew Arnold, eldest son of the late Thomas Arnold, D.D., Head Master of Rugby School. Born December 24, 1822. Died April 15, 1888. 'There is sprung up a light for the righteous, and joyful gladness for such as are true-hearted.'"

ces Lucy Arnold. Born October 15, 1853. Died February 16, 1872. In the morning it is green and groweth up." Near by are other tombstones bearing the name of Arnold — the dates inscribed on them referring to about the beginning of this century. These mark the resting-place of some of the poet's kindred. His father, the famous Dr. Arnold of Rugby, rests in Rugby chapel — that noble father, that true friend and servant of humanity, of whom the son wrote those memorable words of imperishable nobility and meaning, "Thou, my father, wouldst not be saved alone." Matthew Arnold himself is buried in the same grave with his eldest son and side by side with his little children. He who was himself as a little child in his innocence, goodness, and truth, where else and how else could he so fitly rest? "Awake, thou, Lute and Harp! I will awake right early."

Every man will have his own thoughts in such a place as this; will reflect upon his own afflictions, and from knowledge of the manner and spirit in which kindred griefs have been borne by the great heart of intellect and genius will seek to gather strength and patience to endure them well. Matthew Arnold taught many lessons of immense value to those who are able to think. He did not believe that happiness is the destiny of the human race on earth, or that there is a visible ground for assuming that happiness in this mortal condition is one of the inherent rights of humanity. He did not think that this world is made an abode of delight by the mere jocular affirmation that everything in it is well and lovely. He knew better than that. But his message, delivered in poetic strains that will endure as long as our language exists, is the message, not of gloom and despair, but of spiritual purity and sweet and gentle patience. The man who heeds Matthew Arnold's teaching will put no trust in creeds and superstitions, will place no reliance upon the cobweb structures of theology, will take no guidance from the animal and unthinking multitude; but he will "keep the whiteness of his soul"; he will be simple, unselfish, and sweet; he will live for the spirit and not the flesh; and in that spirit, pure, tender, fearless, strong to bear and patient to suffer, he will find composure to meet the inevitable disasters of life and the awful mystery of death. Such was the burden of my thought, sitting there, in the gloaming, beside the lifeless dust of him whose hand had once, with kindly greeting, been clasped in mine. And such will be the thought of many and many a pilgrim who will stand in that sacred place, on many a summer evening of the long future —

"While the stars come out and the **night wind**
   Brings, up the stream,
   Murmurs and scents of **the infinite sea.**"

II.

HAUNTED GLENS AND HOUSES.

WARWICK, JULY 6, 1888.—One night about fifty years ago a brutal murder was done at a lonely place on the highroad between Hampton Lucy and Stratford-upon-Avon. The next morning the murdered man (a farmer named Irons) was found lying by the roadside, his mangled head resting in a small hole. The assassins, two in number, were shortly afterward discovered, and they were hanged at Warwick. From that day to this the hole wherein the dead man's head reposed remains unchanged. No matter how often it may be filled, whether by the wash of heavy rains or by stones and leaves that wayfarers may happen to cast into it as they pass, it is soon found to be again empty. No one takes care of it. No one knows whether or by whom it is guarded. Fill it at nightfall and you will find it empty in the morning. That is the local belief and affirmation. This spot is about two miles north of Stratford and not distant from the gates of Charlcote Park. I looked at this hole one bright day in June and saw that it was empty. Nature, it is thought by the poets, abhors complicity with the concealment of crime and brands with her curse the places that are linked with the shedding of blood. Hence that strong line in Tom Hood's poem of *Eugene Aram* —

"And a mighty wind had swept the leaves,
And still the corse was bare."

There are many haunted spots in Warwickshire. The benighted peasant never lingers on Ganerslie Heath — for there, at midnight, dismal bells have been heard to toll from Blacklow Hill, the place where Sir Piers Gaveston, the corrupt, handsome, foreign favourite of King Edward the Second, was beheaded, by order of the grim barons whom he had insulted and opposed. The Earl of Warwick led them, whom Gaveston had called the Black Dog of Arden. This was long ago. Everybody knows the historic incident but no one can so completely realise it as when standing on the place. The scene of the execution is marked by a simple cross, bearing this inscription: "In the hollow of this rock was beheaded, on the first day of July 1312, by Barons lawless as himself, Piers Gaveston, Earl of Cornwall. In life and death a memorable instance of misrule." No doubt the birds were singing and the green branches of the trees were waving in the summer wind on that fatal day, just as they are at this moment. Gaveston was a man of much personal beauty and some talent, and only twenty-nine years old. It was a melancholy sacrifice and horrible in the circumstances that attended it. No wonder that doleful thoughts and blood-curdling sounds should come to such as walk on Ganerslie Heath in the lonely hours of the night.

Another haunted place is Clopton — haunted certainly with memories if not with ghosts. In the reign of Henry VII. this was the manor of Sir Hugh Clopton, Lord Mayor of London, he who built the bridge over the Avon — across which, many a time, William Shakespeare must have ridden, on his way to Oxford and the capital. The dust of Sir Hugh Clopton rests in Stratford church and his mansion has passed through many hands. In our time it is the residence of Sir Arthur Hodgson, by whom it was purchased in 1871. It was my privilege to see Clopton under the guidance of its lord, and a charming and impressive old house it is — full of quaint objects and fraught with singular associations. They show you there, among many fine paintings, the portrait of a wild-eyed lady with thin figure, delicate features, long light hair, and sensitive countenance, who in the far-off Tudor time drowned herself in a dismal well, back of the mansion — one of the many victims, doubtless, of unhappy love. And they show you the portrait of still another Clopton girl, of ancient times, who is thought to have been accidentally buried alive — because when it chanced that the family tomb was opened, a few days after her interment, the corse was found to be turned over in its coffin and to present indications that the wretched victim of premature burial had, in her agonised frenzy, gnawed her own flesh.

It is the blood-stained corridor of Clopton, however, that most impresses imagination. This is at the top of the house, and access to it is gained by a winding stair of oak boards, uncarpeted, solid, simple, and consonant with the times and manners that it represents. Many years

ago, it is said, a man was murdered in a
little bedroom near the top of this staircase, and his body was dragged along
the corridor to be secreted. A thin dark
stain, seemingly a streak of blood, runs
from the door of that bedroom in the direction of the stairhead, and this is so
deeply imprinted in the wood that it cannot be removed. Opening from this corridor, opposite to the murder-room, is an
odd apartment, which in the remote days
of a Catholic occupant was used as an oratory.[1] In the early part of the reign of
Henry VI. John Carpenter obtained from
the Bishop of Worcester permission to establish this chapel. In 1885 the walls of
this chamber were committed to the tender
mercies of a paper-hanger, who presently
discovered on them several inscriptions in
black letter, and who fortunately mentioned
his discoveries before they were obliterated.
Richard Savage, the antiquary, was called
to examine them, and by him they were
restored. The effect of those little patches
of letters — isles of significance in a barren
sea of wall-paper — is that of extreme sin-

---

[1] An entry in the Diocesan Register of Worcester
states that in 1374 John Clopton of Stretforde obtained letters dimissory to the order of priest.

gularity. Most of them are sentences from the Bible. All of them are devout. One imparts the solemn injunction: "Whether you rise yearlye or goe to bed late, Remember Christ Jesus who died for your sake." [This may be found in John Weever's *Funeral Monuments:* 1631.] Clopton has a long and various history. One of the most significant facts in its record is the fact that for about ten months, in the year 1605, it was occupied by Ambrose Rokewood, of Coldham Hall, Suffolk, a breeder of race-horses, whom Robert Catesby brought into the ghastly Gunpowder Plot, in the reign of James I. Hither came Sir Everard Digby, and Tom and Robert Winter, and the specious Jesuit, Father Garnet, chief hatcher of the conspiracy, with his vile train of sentimental fanatics, on that pilgrimage of sanctification with which he formally prepared for an act of such hideous treachery and wholesale murder as only a religious zealot could ever have conceived. That may have been a time when the little oratory of Clopton was in Catholic use. Not many years since it was a bedroom; but one of Sir Arthur Hodgson's guests, who undertook to sleep in it, was afterward heard to declare that he wished not ever again to experience the hospitality of that chamber, because the sounds that he had heard all around the place throughout that night were of a most infernal description. A house containing many rooms and staircases, a house full of long corridors and winding ways, a house so large that you may readily get lost in it — such is Clopton; and it stands in its own large park, removed from other buildings and bowered in trees. To sit in the great hall of that mansion on a winter midnight, when the snow-laden wind is howling around it, and then to think of the bleak, sinister oratory, and the stealthy, gliding shapes upstairs, invisible to mortal eye, but felt, with a shuddering sense of some unseen presence watching in the dark, — this would be to have quite a sufficient experience of a haunted house. Sir Arthur Hodgson talked of the legends of Clopton with that merry twinkle of the eye which suits well with kindly incredulity. All the same I thought of Milton's lines —

"Millions of spiritual creatures walk the earth
Unseen, both when we wake and when we sleep."

Warwickshire swarmed with conspirators

while the Gunpowder Plot was in progress. The Lion Inn at Dunchurch was the chief tryst of the captains who were to lead their forces and capture the Princess Elizabeth and seize the throne and the country after the expected explosion — which never came. And when the game was up and Fawkes in captivity, it was through Warwickshire that the "racing and chasing" was fleetest and wildest, till the desperate scramble for life and safety went down in blood at Hewel Grange. Various houses associated with that plot are still extant in this neighbourhood, and when the scene shifts to London and to Garnet's Tyburn gallows, it is easily possible for the patient antiquarian to tread in almost every footprint of that great conspiracy.

Since Irish ruffians began to toss dynamite about in public buildings it has been deemed essential to take especial precaution against the danger of explosion in such places as the Houses of Parliament, Westminster Abbey, and the Tower of London. Much more damage than the newspapers recorded was done by the explosions that occurred some time ago in the Tower and the Palace. At present you cannot enter even into Palace Yard unless connected with the public business or authorised by an order; and if you visit the Tower without a special permit you will be restricted to a few sights and places. I was fortunately the bearer of the card of the Lord Chamberlain, on a recent prowl through the Tower, and therefore was favoured by the beef-eaters who pervade that structure. Those damp and gloomy dungeons were displayed wherein so many Jews perished miserably in the reign of Edward I.; and "Little Ease" was shown — the cell in which for several months Guy Fawkes was incarcerated, during Cecil's wily investigation of the Gunpowder Plot. A part of the rear wall has been removed, affording access to the adjacent dungeon; but originally the cell did not give room for a man to lie down in it, and scarce gave room for him to stand upright. The massive door, of ribbed and iron-bound oak, still solid though worn, would make an impressive picture. A poor, stealthy cat was crawling about in those subterranean dens of darkness and horror, and was left locked in there when we emerged. In St. Peter's, on the green — that little cemetery so eloquently described by Macaulay — they came some time ago upon the coffins of Lovat, Kilmarnock, and

Balmerino, the Scotch lords who perished upon the block for their complicity with the rising for Charles Edward Stuart, the Pretender, in 1745-47. The coffins were much decayed. The plates were removed, and these may now be viewed in a glass case on the church wall, just over against the spot where those unfortunate gentlemen were buried.[1] One is of lead and is in the form of a large open scroll. The other two are oval in shape, large, and made of pewter. Much royal and noble dust is heaped together beneath the stones of the chancel — Anne Boleyn, Catherine Howard, Lady Jane Grey, Margaret Duchess of Salisbury, the Duke of Monmouth, the Earl of Northumberland, Essex, Overbury, Thomas Cromwell, and many more. The body of the infamous and execrable Jeffreys was once buried there, but it has been removed.

St. Mary's church at Warwick has been restored since 1885, and now it is made a show place. You see the Beauchamp chapel, in which are entombed Thomas Beauchamp, Earl of Warwick, the founder

---

[1] It is said, however, that the remains of Lord Lovat were secretly removed and buried at his home near Inverness; and that the head was sewed to the body.

of the church; Robert Dudley, Earl of Leicester, in whose Latin epitaph it is stated that "his sorrowful wife, Lætitia, daughter of Francis Knolles, through a sense of conjugal love and fidelity, hath put up this monument to the best and dearest of husbands"; Ambrose Dudley, elder brother to Elizabeth's favourite, and known as the Good Earl (he relinquished his title and possessions to Robert); and that Fulke Greville, Lord Brooke, who lives in fame as "the friend of Sir Philip Sidney." There are other notable sleepers in that chapel, but these perhaps are the most famous and considerable. One odd epitaph records of William Viner, steward to Lord Brooke, that "he was a man entirely of ancient manners, and to whom you will scarcely find an equal, particularly in point of liberality. . . . He was added to the number of the heavenly inhabitants maturely for himself, but permaturely for his friends, in his 70th year, on the 28th of April, A.D. 1639." Another, placed for himself by Thomas Hewett during his lifetime, modestly describes him as "a most miserable sinner." Sin is always miserable when it knows itself. Still another, and this in good verse, by Gervas Clifton, gives a tender tribute to Lætitia ("the excellent and pious Lady Lettice"), Countess of Leicester, who died on Christmas morning, 1634: —

> "She that in her younger years
> Matched with two great English peers;
> She that did supply the wars
> With thunder, and the Court with stars;
> She that in her youth had been
> Darling to the maiden Queene,
> Till she was content to quit
> Her favour for her favourite. . . .
> While she lived she livéd thus,
> Till that God, displeased with us,
> Suffered her at last to fall,
> Not from Him, but from us all."

A noble bust of that fine thinker and exquisite poet Walter Savage Landor has been placed on the west wall of St. Mary's church. He was a native of Warwick and he is fitly commemorated in that place. The bust is of alabaster and is set in an alabaster arch with carved environment, and with the family arms displayed above. The head of Landor shows great intellectual power, rugged yet gentle. Coming suddenly upon the bust, in this church, one is forcibly and pleasantly reminded of the attribute of sweet and gentle reverence in the English character which so invariably expresses itself, all over this land, in honourable memorials to the honourable dead. No rambler in Warwick omits to explore Leicester's hospital, or to see as much as he can of the Castle. That glorious old place has long been kept closed for fear of the dynamite fiend; but now it is once more accessible. I walked again beneath the stately cedars and along the bloom-bordered avenues where once Joseph Addison used to wander and meditate, and traversed again those opulent state apartments wherein so many royal, noble, and beautiful faces look forth from the radiant canvas of Holbein and Vandyke. There is a wonderful picture, in one of those rooms, of Thomas Wentworth, Earl of Strafford, when a young man — a face prophetic of stormy life and baleful struggles and a hard and miserable fate. You may see the helmet that was worn by Oliver Cromwell, and also a striking death-mask of his face. The finest portraits of King Charles I. that exist in this kingdom are shown at Warwick Castle.

III.

OLD YORK.

YORK, August 12, 1888. — All summer long the sorrowful skies have been weeping over England, and my first prospect of this ancient city was a prospect through drizzle and mist. Yet even so it was impressive. York is one of the quaintest cities in the kingdom. Many of the streets are narrow and crooked. Most of the buildings are of low stature, built of brick, and roofed with red tiles. Here and there you find a house of Queen Elizabeth's time, picturesque with overhanging timber-crossed fronts and peaked gables. One such house, in Stonegate, is conspicuously marked with its date, 1574. Another, in College street, enclosing a quadrangular court and lovely with old timber and carved gateway, was built by the Neville family in 1460. There is a wide area in the centre of the town called Parliament street, where the market is opened by torchlight on certain evenings of every week. It was market-time last evening, and, wandering through the motley and merry crowd that filled the square, about nine o'clock, I bought at a flower-stall the white rose of York and the red rose of Lancaster — twining them together as an emblem of the settled peace that here broods so sweetly over the venerable relics of a wild and stormy past.

Four sections of the old wall of York are still extant and the observer is amused to perceive the ingenuity with which these gray and mouldering remnants of the feudal age are blended into the structures of the democratic present. From Bootham to Monk Gate (so named in honour of General Monk at the Restoration), a distance of about half a mile, the wall is absorbed by the adjacent buildings. But you may walk upon it from Monk Gate to Jewbury, about a quarter of a mile, and afterward, crossing the Foss, you may find it again on the southeast of the city, and walk upon it from Red Tower to old Fishergate, descending near York Castle. There are houses both within the walls and without. The walk is about eight feet wide, protected on one hand by a fretted battlement and on the other by an occasional bit of iron fence. The base of the wall, for a considerable part of its extent, is fringed with market gardens or with grassy banks. In one of its towers there is a gate-house, still occupied as a dwelling; and a comfortable dwelling no doubt it is. In another, of which nothing now remains but the walls, four large trees are rooted; and as they are already tall enough to wave their leafy tops above the battlement they must have been growing there for twenty years. At one point the Great Northern Railway enters through an arch in the ancient wall, and as you look down from the battlements your gaze rests upon long lines of rail and a spacious station — together with its adjacent hotel; objects which consort but strangely with what your fancy knows of York; a city of donjons and barbicans, the moat, the drawbridge, the portcullis, the citadel, the man-at-arms, and the knight in armour, with the banners of William the Norman flowing over all.

The river Ouse divides the city of York, which lies mostly upon its east bank, and in order to reach the longest and most attractive portion of the wall that is now available to the pedestrian you must cross the Ouse either at Skeldergate or Lendal, paying a halfpenny as toll, both when you go and when you return. The walk here is three-quarters of a mile long, and from an angle of this wall, just above the railway arch, may be obtained the best view of the mighty cathedral — one of the most stupendous and sublime works that ever were erected by the inspired brain and loving labour of man. While I walked there last night, and mused upon the story of the Wars of the Roses, and strove to conjure up the pageants and the horrors that must have been presented all about this region in that remote and turbulent past, the glorious bells of the minster were chiming from its towers, while the fresh evening breeze, sweet with the fragrance of wet flowers and foliage, seemed to flood this ancient, venerable city with the golden music of a celestial benediction.

The pilgrim to York stands in the centre of the largest shire in England and is surrounded with castles and monasteries, now mostly in ruins but teeming with those associations of history and literature that are the glory of this delightful land. From the summit of the great central tower of the cathedral, which is reached by two hundred and thirty-seven steps, I gazed out over the vale of York and beheld one of the loveliest spectacles that ever blessed the eyes of man. The wind was fierce, the sun brilliant, and the vanquished storm-clouds were streaming away before the northern blast. Far beneath lay the red-roofed city, its devious lanes and its many gray churches — crumbling relics of ancient ecclesiastical power — distinctly visible. Through the plain, and far away toward the south and east, ran the silver thread of the Ouse, while all around, as far as the eye could reach, stretched forth a smiling landscape of emerald meadow and cultivated field; here a patch of woodland, and there a silver gleam of wave; here a manor-house nestled amid stately trees, and there an ivy-covered fragment of ruined masonry; and everywhere the green lines of the flowering hedge. The prospect is finer here than even it is from the summit of Strasburg cathedral; and indeed, when all is said that can be said about natural scenery and architectural sublimities, it seems amazing that any lover of the beautiful should deem it necessary to quit the infinite variety of the British islands. Earth cannot show you anything more softly fair than the lakes and mountains of Cumberland and

Westmoreland. No city can excel Edinburgh in stately solidity of character or tranquil grandeur, or in magnificence of position. The most exquisitely beautiful of churches is Roslin chapel. And though you search the wide world through you will never find such cathedrals — so fraught with majesty, sublimity, the loveliness of human art, and the ecstatic sense of a divine element in human destiny! — as those of York, Canterbury, Gloucester, and Lincoln. While thus I lingered in wondering meditation upon the crag-like summit of York minster, the muffled thunder of its vast, sonorous organ rose, rolling and throbbing, from the mysterious depth below, and seemed to shake the great tower as with a mighty blast of jubilation and worship. At such moments, if ever, when the tones of human adoration are floating up to heaven, a man is lifted out of himself and made to forget his puny mortal existence and all the petty nothings that weary his spirit, darken his vision, and weigh him down to the level of the sordid, trivial world. Well did they know this — those old monks who built the abbeys of Britain, laying their foundations not alone deeply in the earth but deeply in the human soul!

All the ground that you survey from the top of York minster is classic ground — at least to those persons whose imaginations are kindled by associations with the stately and storied past. In the city that lies at your feet stood once the great Constantine, to be proclaimed emperor and to be invested with the imperial purple of Rome. In the original York minster — for the present is the fourth church that has been erected upon this site — was buried that valiant soldier "Old Siward," whom "gracious England" lent to the Scottish cause, under Malcolm and Macduff, when time at length was ripe for the ruin of Glamis and Cawdor. Close by is the field of Stamford bridge, where Harold defeated the Danes, with terrible slaughter, only nine days before he himself was defeated and slain at Hastings. Southward, following the line of the Ouse, you look down upon the ruins of Clifford's Tower, built by William the Conqueror, in 1068, and destroyed by the explosion of its powder magazine in 1684. Not far away is the battlefield of Towton, where the great Warwick slew his horse that he might fight on foot and possess no advantage over the common soldiers of his force. Henry VI. and Margaret were waiting in York for news of the event of that fatal battle — which, in its effect, made them exiles and bore to an assured supremacy the rightful standard of the White Rose. In this church Edward IV. was crowned and Richard III. was proclaimed king and had his second coronation. Southward you may see the open space called the Pavement, connecting with Parliament street, and the red brick church of St. Crux. In the Pavement the Earl of Northumberland was beheaded for treason against Queen Elizabeth in 1572, and in St. Crux (one of Wren's churches) his remains lie buried, beneath a dark blue slab, still shown to visitors. A few miles away, but easily within reach of your vision, is the field of Marston Moor, where the impetuous Prince Rupert imperilled and well-nigh lost the cause of Charles I. in 1644; and as you look toward that fatal spot you can almost hear, in the chamber of your fancy, the pæans of thanksgiving for the victory that were uttered in the church beneath. Cromwell, then a subordinate officer in the Parliamentary army, was one of the worshippers. Charles also has knelt at this altar. Indeed, of the fifteen kings, from William of Normandy to Henry of

Windsor, whose sculptured effigies appear upon the chancel screen in York minster, there is scarcely one who has not worshipped in this cathedral.

York minster has often been described, but no description can convey an adequate impression of its grandeur. Canterbury is the lovelier cathedral of the two — though not the grander — and Canterbury possesses the inestimable advantage of a spacious close. It must be said also, for the city of Canterbury, that the presence and influence of a great church are more distinctly and delightfully felt in that place than they are in York. There is a more spiritual tone at Canterbury, a tone of superior delicacy and refinement, a certain aristocratic coldness and repose. In York you perceive the coarse spirit of a democratic era. The walls, that ought to be cherished with scrupulous care, are found in many places to be defiled. At intervals along the walks upon the banks of the Ouse you behold placards requesting the co-operation of the public in protecting from harm the swans that navigate the river. Even in the cathedral itself there is displayed a printed notice that the Dean and Chapter are amazed at disturbances which occur in the nave while

divine service is proceeding in the choir.
These things imply a rough element in the
population, and in such a place as York
such an element is exceptionally offensive
and deplorable.

It was said by the late Lord Beaconsfield
that progress in the nineteenth century is
found to consist chiefly in a return to ancient
ideas. There may be places to which
the characteristic spirit of the present day
contributes an element of beauty; but if so
I have not seen them. Wherever there is
beauty there is the living force of tradition
to account for it. The most that a conservative
force in society can accomplish,
for the preservation of an instinct in favour
of whatever is beautiful and impressive, is
to protect what remains from the past.
Modern Edinburgh, for example, has contributed
no building that is comparable
with its glorious old castle, or with Roslin,
or with what we know to have been Melrose
and Dryburgh; but its castle and its
chapels are protected and preserved. York,
in the present day, erects a commodious
railway-station and a sumptuous hotel, and
spans its ample river with two splendid
bridges; but its modern architecture is
puerile beside that of its ancient minster;

and so its best work, after all, is the preservation of its cathedral. One finds it difficult to understand how anybody, however lowly born or poorly endowed or meanly nurtured, can live within the presence of that heavenly building, and not be purified and exalted by the contemplation of so much majesty, and by its constantly irradiative force of religious sentiment and power. But the spirit which in the past created objects of beauty and adorned common life with visible manifestations of the celestial aspiration in human nature had constantly to struggle against insensibility or violence; and just so the few who have inherited that spirit in the present day are compelled steadily to combat the hard materialism and gross animal proclivities of the new age.

What a comfort their souls must find in such an edifice as York minster! What a solace and what an inspiration! There it stands, dark and lonely to-night, but symbolising, as no other object upon earth can ever do, except one of its own great kindred, God's promise of immortal life to man and man's unquenchable faith in the promise of God. Dark and lonely now, but during many hours of its daily and nightly life sentient, eloquent, vital, participating in all the thought and conduct and experience of those who dwell around it. The beautiful peal of its bells that I heard last night was for Canon Baillie, one of the oldest and most beloved and venerated of its clergy. This morning, sitting in its choir, I heard the tender, thoughtful eulogy so simply and sweetly spoken by the aged Dean, and once again learned the essential lesson that an old age of grace, patience, and benignity means a pure heart, an unselfish spirit, and a good life passed in the service of others. This afternoon I had a place among the worshippers that thronged the nave to hear the special anthem chanted for the deceased Canon; and, as the organ pealed forth its mellow thunder, and the rich tones of the choristers swelled and rose and broke in golden waves of melody upon the groined arches and vaulted roof, my soul seemed borne away to a peace and rest that are not of this world. To-night the rising moon, as she gleams through drifting clouds, will pour her silver rays upon that great east window — at once the largest and the most beautiful in existence — and all the Bible stories told there in such exquisite hues and forms will glow with heavenly lustre on the dark vista of chancel and nave. And when the morning comes the first beams of the rising sun will stream through the great casement and illumine the figures of saints and archbishops, and gild the old tattered battle-flags in the chancel aisle, and touch with blessing the marble effigies of the dead; and we who walk there, refreshed and comforted, shall feel that the vast cathedral is indeed the gateway to heaven.

York minster is the loftiest of all the English cathedrals, and the second in length — Winchester being thirty feet longer. The present structure is six hundred years old, and two hundred years were occupied in the building of it. They show you, in the crypt, some fine remains of the Norman church that preceded it upon the same site, together with traces of the still older Saxon church that preceded the Norman. The first one was of wood and was totally destroyed. The Saxon remains are a fragment of stone staircase and a piece of wall built in the ancient "herring-bone" fashion. The Norman remains are four clustered columns, embellished in the dog-tooth style. There is not much of commemorative statuary at York minster, and what there is of it was placed chiefly in the chancel. Archbishop Scrope, who figures in Shakespeare's historical play of *Henry IV.*, was buried in the lady chapel. Laurence Sterne's grandfather, who was chaplain to Laud, is represented there, in his ecclesiastic dress, reclining upon a couch and supporting his mitred head upon his hand — a squat figure uncomfortably posed, but sculptured with delicate skill. Many historic names occur in the inscriptions — Wentworth, Finch, Fenwick, Carlisle, and Heneage, — and in the north aisle of the chancel is the tomb of William of Hatfield, second son of Edward III., who died in 1343–44, in the eighth year of his age. An alabaster statue of the royal boy reclines upon his tomb. In the cathedral library, which contains eight thousand volumes and is kept at the Deanery, is the Princess Elizabeth's prayer-book, containing her autograph. In one of the chapels is the original throne-chair of Edward III.

In St. Leonard's Place still stands the York theatre, erected by Tate Wilkinson in 1765. In York Castle Eugene Aram was imprisoned and suffered. Knaresborough, the scene of his crime, is but a few miles distant. The poet Porteous, the sculptor Flaxman, and the fanatic Guy Fawkes, were natives of York, and have often walked its streets. Standing on Skeldergate bridge, few readers of English fiction could fail to recall that exquisite description of the place in the novel of *No Name*. In his artistic use of weather, atmosphere, and colour Wilkie Collins is always remarkable equally for his fidelity to nature and fact, and for the felicity and beauty of his language. His portrayal of York seems more than ever a gem of literary art, when you have seen the veritable spot of poor Magdalen's meeting with Captain Wragge. The name of Wragge is on one of the signboards in the city. The river, on which I did not omit to take a boat, was picturesque, with its many quaint barges, bearing masts and sails and embellished with touches of green and crimson and blue. There is no end to the associations and suggestions of the storied city. But you are weary of them by this time. Let me respect the admonition of the midnight bell, and seek repose beneath the hospitable wing of the old Black Swan in Coney street, whence I send this humble memorial of ancient York.

IV.

THE HAUNTS OF MOORE.

DEVIZES, WILTSHIRE, August 20, 1888.
— The scarlet discs of the poppies and the red and white blooms of the clover, together with wild-flowers of many hues, bespangle now the emerald sod of England, while the air is rich with fragrance of lime-trees and of new-mown hay. The busy and sagacious rooks, fat and bold, wing their way in great clusters, bent on forage and mischief. There is almost a frosty chill in the autumnal air, and the brimming rivers, dark and deep and smoothly flowing through the opulent, cultivated, and park-like region of Wiltshire, look cold and bright. In many fields the hay is cut and stacked. In others the men, and often the women, armed with rakes, are tossing it to dry in the reluctant, intermittent, bleak sunshine of this rigorous August. Overhead the sky is now as blue as the deep sea and now grim and ominous with great drifting masses of

slate-coloured cloud. There are moments of beautiful sunshine by day, and in some hours of the night the moon shines forth in all her pensive and melancholy glory. It is a time of exquisite loveliness, and it has seemed a fitting time for a visit to the last English home and the last resting-place of the poet of loveliness and love, the great Irish poet Thomas Moore.

When Moore first went up to London, a young author seeking to launch his earliest writings upon the stream of contemporary literature, he crossed from Dublin to Bristol and then travelled to the capital by way of Bath and Devizes; and as he crossed several times he must soon have gained familiarity with this part of the country. He did not, however, settle in Wiltshire until some years afterward. His first lodging in London was a front room, up two pair of stairs, at No. 44 George Street, Portman Square. He subsequently lived at No. 46 Wigmore Street, Cavendish Square, and at No. 27 Bury Street, St. James's. This was in 1805. In 1810 he resided for a time at No. 22 Molesworth Street, Dublin, but he soon returned to England. One of his homes, shortly after his marriage with Elizabeth Dyke ("Bessie," the sister of the great actress Mary Duff) was in Brompton. In the spring of 1812 he settled at Kegworth, but a year later he is found at Mayfield Cottage, near Ashbourne, Derbyshire. "I am now as you wished," he wrote to Mr. Power, the music-publisher, July 1, 1813, "within twenty-four hours' drive of town." In 1817 he occupied a cottage near the foot of Muswell Hill, at Hornsey, Middlesex, but after he lost his daughter Barbara, who died there, the place became distressful to him and he left it. In the latter part of September that year, the time of their affliction, Moore and his Bessie were the guests of Lady Donegal at No. 56 Davies Street, Berkeley Square, London. Then they removed to Sloperton Cottage, at Bromham, near Devizes (November 19, 1817), and their permanent residence was established in that place. Lord Lansdowne, one of the poet's earliest and best friends, was the owner of this estate, and doubtless he was the impulse of Moore's resort to it. The present Lord Lansdowne still owns Bowood Park, about four miles away.

Devizes impresses you with the singular sense of being a place in which something is always about to happen; but nothing ever does happen in it, or ever will. Quieter it could not be unless it were dead. The principal street in it runs nearly northwest and southeast. There is a Northgate at one end of it and a Southgate at the other. Most of the streets are narrow and crooked. The houses are low, and built of brick. Few buildings are pretentious. A canal intersects the place, but in such a subterranean and furtive manner as scarcely to attract even casual notice. Public-houses are sufficiently numerous and they appear to be sufficiently prosperous. Even while I write, the voice of song, issuing somewhat discordantly from one of them in this immediate neighbourhood, declares, with beery emphasis, that "Britons never, never, never will be slaves." Close by stands a castle — a new one, built, however, upon the basis and plan of an ancient structure that was long included in the dowry settled upon successive Queens of England. In the centre of the town is a large square, which only needs a fringe of well-grown trees to make it exceedingly pleasant — for its commodious expanse is seldom invaded by a vehicle or a human being. Pilgrims in quest of peace could not do better than to tarry here. Nobody is in a hurry about anything and manners are primitive and frank.

The city bell which officially strikes the hours in Devizes is subdued and thoughtful, and although furnished with chimes it always speaks under its breath. The church-bell, however, rings long and heartily and with a melodious clangour — as though the local sinners were more than commonly hard of hearing. In the public square there are two works of art — one a fountain, the other a market cross. The latter, a good specimen of the perpendicular Gothic, has thirteen spires, rising above an arched canopy for a statue. One face of it is inscribed as follows: "This Market Cross was erected by Henry Viscount Sidmouth, as a memorial of his grateful attachment to the Borough of Devizes, of which he has been Recorder thirty years, and of which he was six times unanimously chosen a representative in Parliament. Anno Domini 1814." Upon the other face appears a record vastly more significant — being indicative, as to the city fathers, equally of credulity and a frugal mind, and being in itself freighted with tragic import unmatched since the Bible narrative of Ananias and Sapphira. It reads thus: —

"The Mayor and Corporation of Devizes avail themselves of the stability of this building to transmit to future times the record of an awful event which occurred in this market-place in the year 1753, hoping that such a record may serve as a salutary warning against the danger of impiously invoking the Divine vengeance, or of calling on the holy name of God to conceal the devices of falsehood and fraud.

"On Thursday, the 25th January 1753, Ruth Pierce, of Potterne, in this county, agreed, with three other women, to buy a sack of wheat in the market, each paying her due proportion toward the same.

"One of these women, in collecting the several quotas of money, discovered a deficiency, and demanded of Ruth Pierce the sum which was wanted to make good the amount.

"Ruth Pierce protested that she had paid her share, and said, 'She wished she might drop down dead if she had not.'

"She rashly repeated this awful wish, when, to the consternation of the surrounding multitude, she instantly fell down and expired, having the money concealed in her hand."

An interesting church in Devizes is that of St. John, the Norman tower of which is a relic of the days of King Henry II., a vast, grim structure with a circular turret on one corner of it. Eastward of this church is a long and lovely avenue of trees, and around it lies a large burial-place, remarkable for the excellence of the sod and for the number visible of those heavy, gray, oblong masses of tombstone which appear to have obtained great public favour about the time of Cromwell. In the centre of the churchyard stands a monolith, inscribed with these words:—

"Remember the Sabbath-day to keep it holy.—This monument, as a solemn monitor to Young People to remember their Creator in the days of their youth, was erected by subscription.—In memory of the sudden and awful end of Robert Merrit and his wife, Eliz. Tiley, her sister, Martha Carter, and Josiah Denham, who were drowned, in the flower of their youth, in a pond, near this town, called Drews, on Sunday evening, the 30th of June, 1751, and are together underneath entombed."

In one corner of the churchyard I came upon a cross, bearing a simple legend far more solemn, sensible, touching, and admonitory: "In Memoriam — Robert Samuel Thornley. Died August 5, 1871. Aged 48 years. For fourteen years surgeon to the poor of Devizes. 'There shall be no more pain.'" And over still another sleeper was written, upon a flat stone, low in the ground —

"Loving, beloved, in all relations true,
 Exposed to follies, but subdued by few:

Reader, reflect, and copy if you can
The simple virtues of this honest man."

As I was gazing at one of the old churches, surrounded with many ponderous tombstones and looking gray and cheerless in the gloaming, an old man approached me and civilly began a conversation about the antiquity of the church and the eloquence of its rector. When I told him that I had walked to Bromham to attend the service there, and to see the cottage and grave of Moore, he presently furnished to me that little touch of personal testimony which is always so interesting and significant in such circumstances. "I remember Tom Moore," he said; "I saw him when he was alive. I worked for him once in his house, and I did some work once on his tomb. He was a little man. He spoke to us very pleasantly. I don't think he was a preacher. He never preached that I heard tell of. He was a poet, I believe. He was very much liked here. No, I never heard a word against him. I am seventy-nine years old the 13th of December, and that'll soon be here. I've had three wives in my time, and my third is still living. It's a fine old church, and there's figures in it of bishops, and kings, and queens."

Most observers have remarked the odd way, garrulous, and sometimes unconsciously humorous, in which senile persons prattle their incongruous and sporadic recollections. But — "How pregnant sometimes his replies are!" Another resident of Devizes, with whom I conversed, likewise remembered the poet, and spoke of him with affectionate regard. "My sister, when she was a child," he said, "was often at Moore's house, and he was fond of her. Yes, his name is widely remembered and honoured here. But I think that many of the poor people hereabout, the farmers, admired him chiefly because they thought that he wrote Moore's Almanac. They often used to say to him: 'Mister Moore, please tell us what the weather's going to be.'"

From Devizes to the village of Bromham, a distance of about four miles, the walk is delightful. Much of the path is between green hedges and is embowered by elms. The exit from the town is by Northgate and along the Chippenham road — which, like all the roads in this neighbourhood, is smooth, hard, and white. A little way out of Devizes, going northwest, this road makes a deep cut in the chalk-stone and so winds down hill into the level plain. At intervals you come upon sweetly pretty specimens of the English thatch-roof cottage. Hay-fields, pastures, and market-gardens extend on every hand. Eastward, far off, are visible the hills of Westbury, upon which, here and there, the copses are lovely, and upon one of which, cut in the rock, is the figure of a colossal white horse — said to have been put there by the Saxons to commemorate the victories of King Alfred. Soon the road winds over a hill and you pass through the little red village of Rowde, with its gray church-tower. The walk may be shortened by a cut across the fields, and this indeed is found the sweetest part of the journey — for now the path lies through gardens, and through the centre or along the margin of the wheat, which waves in the strong wind and sparkles in the bright sunshine and is everywhere tenderly touched with the scarlet of the poppy and with hues of other wild-flowers — making you think of Shakespeare's

"Rank fumiter and furrow weeds,
   With hemlock, harlock, nettles, cuckoo-
      flowers,
   Darnel, and all the idle weeds that grow
   In our sustaining corn."

There is one field through which I passed, just as the spire of Bromham church came into view, in which a surface more than three hundred yards square was blazing with wild-flowers, white and gold and crimson and purple and blue, upon a growth of vivid green, so that to look upon it was almost to be dazzled, while the air that floated over it was scented as if with honeysuckle. You may see the delicate spire and the low gray tower of Moore's church some time before you come to it, and in some respects the prospect is not unlike that of Shakespeare's church at Stratford. A sweeter spot for a poet's sepulchre it would be hard to find. No spot could be more harmonious than this one is with the gentle, romantic spirit of Moore's poetry, and with the purity, refinement, and serenity of his life. Bromham village consists of a few red brick buildings, scattered along a few irregular little lanes, on a ridge overlooking a valley. Amid these humble homes stands the gray church, like a shepherd keeping his flock. A part of it is very old, and all of it, richly weather-stained and delicately browned with fading moss, is beautiful. Upon the tower and along the south side the fantastic gargoyles are much decayed. The building is a cross. The chancel window faces eastward, and the window at the end of the nave looks toward the west — the latter being a memorial to Moore. At the southeast corner of the building is the lady chapel, in which are suspended various fragments of old armour, and in the centre of which, recumbent on a great dark tomb, is a grim-visaged knight, clad from top to toe in his mail, beautifully sculptured in marble that looks like yellow ivory. Other tombs are adjacent, with inscriptions that implicate the names of Sir Edward Bayntun, 1679, and Lady Anne Wilmot, elder daughter and coheiress of John, Earl of Rochester, who successively was the wife of Henry Bayntun and Francis Greville, and who died in 1703. The window at the end of the nave is a simple but striking composition, in stained glass, richer and nobler than is commonly seen in a country church. It consists of twenty-one lights, of which five are lancet shafts, side by side, these being surmounted with smaller lancets, forming a cluster at the top of the arch. In the centre is the figure of Jesus and around Him are the Apostles. The colouring is soft, true, and beautiful. Across the base of the window appear the words, in the glass: "This window is placed in this church by the combined subscriptions of two hundred persons who honour the memory of the poet of all circles and the idol of his own, Thomas Moore." It was beneath this window, in a little pew in the corner of the church, that the present writer joined in the service, and meditated, throughout a long sermon, on the lovely life and character and the gentle, noble, and abiding influence of the poet whose hallowed grave and beloved memory make this place a perpetual shrine.

Moore was buried in the churchyard. An iron fence encloses his tomb, which is at the base of the church tower, in an angle formed by the tower and the chancel, on the north side of the building. Not more than twenty tombs are visible on this side of the church, and these appear upon a level lawn as green and sparkling as an emerald and as soft as velvet. On three sides the churchyard is enclosed by a low wall, and on the fourth by a dense hedge of glistening holly. Great trees are all around the church, but not too near. A massive yew stands darkly at one corner. Chestnuts and elms blend their branches in fraternal embrace. Close by the poet's grave a vast beech uprears its dome of fruited boughs and rustling foliage. The sky was blue, except for a few straggling masses of fleecy and slate-coloured cloud. Not a human creature was anywhere to be seen while I stood in this sacred spot, and no sound disturbed the Sabbath stillness, save the faint whisper of the wind in the lofty tree-tops and the low twitter of birds in their hidden nests. I thought of his long life, unblemished by personal guilt or public error; of his sweet devotion to parents and wife and children; of his pure patriotism, which scorned equally the blatant fustian of the demagogue and the frenzy of the revolutionist; of his unsurpassed fidelity in friendship; of his simplicity and purity in a corrupt time and amid many temptations; of his meekness in affliction; of the devout spirit that made him murmur on his deathbed, "Bessie, trust in God"; of the many beautiful songs that he added to our literature,— every one of which is the perfectly melodious and absolutely final expression of one or another of the elemental feelings of human nature; and of the obligation of endless gratitude that the world owes to his fine and high and beneficent genius.

And thus it seemed good to be in this place and to lay with reverent hands the white roses of honour and affection upon his tomb.

On the long, low, flat stone that covers the poet's dust are inscribed the following words: "Anastatia Mary Moore. Born March 16, 1813. Died March 8, 1829. Also her brother, John Russell Moore, who died November 23, 1842, aged 19 years. Also their father, Thomas Moore, tenderly beloved by all who knew the goodness of his heart. The Poet and Patriot of his Country, Ireland. Born May 28, 1779. Sank to rest February 25, 1852. Aged 72. God is Love. Also his wife, Bessie Moore, who died 4th September 1865. And to the memory of their dear son, Thomas Lansdowne Parr Moore. Born 24th October 1818. Died in Africa, January 1846." Moore's little daughter, Barbara, is buried at Hornsey, near London, in the same churchyard where rest the bones of the poet Samuel Rogers. On the stone that marks that spot is written, "Anne Jane Barbara Moore. Born January the 4th, 1812. Died September the 18th, 1817."

Northwest from Bromham church and about one mile away stands Sloperton Cottage, the last home of the poet and the house in which he died. A deep valley intervenes between the church and the cottage, but, as each is built upon a ridge, you may readily see the one from the other. There is a road across the valley, but the more pleasant walk is along a pathway through the meadows and over several stiles, ending almost in front of the storied house. It is an ideal home for a poet. The building is made of brick but it is so completely enwrapped in ivy that scarcely a particle of its surface can be seen. It is a low building, with three gables on its main front and with a wing; it stands in the middle of a garden enclosed by walls and by hedges of ivy; and it is embowered by great trees, yet not so closely embowered as to be shorn of the prospect from its windows. Flowers and flowering vines were blooming around it. The hard, white road, flowing past its gateway, looked like a thread of silver between the green hedgerows which here for many miles are rooted in high, grassy banks, and at intervals are diversified with large trees. Sloperton Cottage is almost alone, but there are a few neighbours and there is a little rustic village about half a mile westward. Westward was the poet's favourite prospect. He loved the sunset, and from a certain terrace in his garden he rarely failed to watch the pageant of the dying day. Here, for thirty-five years, was his peaceful and happy home. Here he meditated many of those gems of lyrical poetry that will live in the hearts of men as long as anything lives that ever was written by mortal hand. And here he "sank to rest," worn out at last by incessant labour and by many sorrows — the bitter fruit of domestic bereavement and disappointment. The sun was sinking as I turned away from this hallowed haunt of genius and virtue, and, through green pastures and flower-spangled fields of waving grain, set forth upon my homeward walk. Soon there was a lovely peal of chimes from Bromham church tower, answered far off by the bells of Rowde, and, while I descended into the darkening valley, Moore's tender words came singing through my thought: —

"And so 'twill be when I am gone —
That tuneful peal will still ring on,
While other bards shall walk these dells
And sing your praise, sweet evening bells!"

V.

BEAUTIFUL BATH.

FROM Devizes the traveller naturally turns toward Bath, which is only a few miles distant. A beautiful city, marred somewhat by the feverish, disturbing spirit of the present day, this old place — in which the Saxon King Edgar was crowned, A.D. 973 — nevertheless retains many interesting characteristics of its former glory. More than a century has passed since the wigged, powdered, and jewelled days of Beau Nash. The Avon (for there is another Avon here, distinct from that of Warwickshire and that of Yorkshire) is spanned by bridges that Smollett never dreamed of and Sheridan never saw. The town has crept upward, along both the valley slopes, nearer and nearer to the hill-tops that used to look down upon it. Along the margins of the river many gray, stone structures are mouldering in neglect and decay; but a tramcar rattles through the principal street;

the bootblack and the newsvender are active and vociferous; the causeways are crowded with a bustling throng, and carts and carriages dash and scramble over the pavement, while, where of old the horn used to sound a gay flourish and the coach to come spinning in from London, now is heard the shriek and clangour of the steam-engine dashing down the vale with morning papers and with passengers, three hours from town. This, indeed, is not "the season" (August 21, 1888), and of late it has rained with zealous persistence, so that Bath is not in her splendour. Much however can be seen, and the essential fact that she is no longer the Gainsborough belle that she used to be is distinctly evident. You must yield your mind to fancy if you would conjure up, while walking in these modern streets, the gay and quaint things described in *Humphrey Clinker* or indicated in *The Rivals*. The Bath chairs, sometimes pulled by donkeys, and sometimes trundled by men, are among the most representative relics now to be seen. Next to the theatre (where it was my privilege to enjoy and admire John L. Toole's richly humorous performance of *The Don*) stands a building, just at the foot of Gascoigne

Place, before which the traveller pauses with interest, because upon its front he may read the legend, neatly engraved on a white marble slab, that "In this house lived the celebrated Beau Nash, and here he died, February 1761." It is an odd structure, consisting of two stories and an attic, the front being of the monotonous stucco that came in with the Regent. Earlier no doubt the building was timbered. There are eleven windows in the front, four of them being painted on the wall. The house is used now by an auctioneer. In the historic Pump Room — dating back to 1797 — raised aloft in an alcove at the east end, still stands the effigy of the Beau, even as it stood in the days when he set the fashions, regulated the customs, and gave the laws, and was the King of Bath; but the busts of Newton and Pope that formerly stood on either side of this statue stand there no more — save in the fancy of those who recall the epigram which was suggested by that singular group: —

> "This statue placed these busts between
> Gives satire all its strength;
> Wisdom and Wit are little seen,
> But Folly at full length."

Folly, though, is a word that carries a

different meaning to different ears. Douglas Jerrold made a play on the subject of Beau Nash — an ingenious, effective, brilliantly written play, in which he is depicted as anything but foolish. Much always depends on the point of view.

Quin was buried in Bath Abbey, and Bath is the scene of *The Rivals*. It would be pleasant to fancy the trim figure of the truculent Sir Lucius O'Trigger strutting along the Parade; or bluff and choleric Sir Anthony Absolute gazing with imperious condescension upon the galaxy of the Pump Room; Acres in his absurd finery; Lydia with her sentimental novels; and Mrs. Malaprop, rigid with decorum, in her Bath chair. The Abbey, begun in 1405 and completed in 1606, has a noble west front and a magnificent door of carved oak, and certainly it is a superb church; but the eyes that have rested upon such cathedrals as those of Durham, Edinburgh, and Glasgow, such a heavenly jewel as Roslin, and such an astounding and overwhelming edifice as York minster, can dwell calmly on Bath Abbey. A surprising feature in it is its mural record of the dead that are entombed beneath or around it. Sir Lucius might well declare that "There is snug lying in the Abbey." Almost every foot of the walls is covered with monumental slabs, and like Captain Cuttle, after the wedding of Mr. Dombey and Edith Granger, I "pervaded the church and read the epitaphs," — solicitous to discover that of the renowned actor James Quin. His tablet was formerly to be found in the chancel, but now it is obscurely placed in a porch, on the north corner of the building, on what may be termed the outer wall of the sanctuary. It presents the face of the famous comedian carved in white marble and set against a black slab. Beneath is the date of his death, "Ob. MDCCLXVI. Aetat LXXIII.," and his epitaph, written by David Garrick. At the base are dramatic emblems — the mask and the dagger. As a portrait this medallion of Quin bears internal evidence of scrupulous fidelity to nature, and certainly it is a fine work of art. The head is dressed as it was in life, with the full wig of the period. The features are delicately cut and are indicative of austere beauty of countenance — impressive if not attractive. The mouth is especially handsome — the upper lip being a perfect Cupid's bow. The face is serious, expressive, and fraught with intellect and power. This was the last great declaimer of the old school of acting, discomfited and almost obliterated by Garrick; and here are the words that Garrick wrote upon his tomb: —

" That tongue which set the table on a roar
  And charmed the public ear is heard no more;
  Closed are those eyes, the harbingers of wit,
  Which spoke, before the tongue, what Shakespeare writ;
  Cold is that hand which, living, was stretched forth,
  At friendship's call, to succour modest worth.
  Here lies JAMES QUIN. Deign, reader, to be taught
  Whate'er thy strength of body, force of thought,
  In nature's happiest mould however cast,
  To this complexion thou must come at last."

A printed reminder of mortality is superfluous in Bath, for you almost continually behold afflicted and deformed persons who have come here to "take the waters." For rheumatic sufferers this place is a paradise — as, indeed, it is for all wealthy persons who love luxury. Walter Savage Landor said that the only two cities of Europe in which he could live were Bath and Florence; but that was long ago. When you have walked in Milsom street and Lansdowne Crescent, sailed upon the Avon, observed the Abbey, without and within — for its dusky, weather-stained walls are extremely picturesque — attended the theatre, climbed the hills for the view of the city and the Avon valley, and taken the baths, you will have had a satisfying experience of Bath. The greatest luxury in the place is a swimming tank of mineral water, about forty feet long, by twenty broad, and five feet deep — a tepid pool of most refreshing potency. And the chief curiosity is the ruin of a Roman bath which was discovered and laid bare in 1885. This is built in the form of a rectangular basin of stone, with steps around it, and it was environed with stone chambers that were used as dressing-rooms. The basin is nearly perfect. The work of restoration of this ancient bath is in progress, but the relic will be preserved only as an emblem of the past.

Haynes Bayly, the song-writer, was born in Bath, and there he melodiously recorded that "She wore a wreath of roses," and there he dreamed of dwelling "in marble halls." But Bath is not nearly as rich in literary associations as its neighbour city of Bristol. Chatterton, Southey, Hannah More, Mary Robinson — the actress, the

lovely and unfortunate "Perdita,"— all
these were born in Bristol. Richard Savage,
the poet, died there (1743), and so did John
Hippesley, the comedian, manager, and
farce-writer (1748). St. Mary Redclyffe
church, built in 1292, is still standing there,
of which Chatterton's father was the sexton,
and in the tower of which "the marvellous boy" discovered, according to his ingenious plan of literary imposture, the
original Canynge and Rowley manuscripts.
That famous preacher, the Rev. Robert
Hall (1764-1831), had a church in Bristol.
Southey and Coleridge married sisters, of
the name of Fricker, who resided there, and
the house once occupied by Coleridge is still
extant in the contiguous village of Clevedon
— one of the loveliest places on the English
coast. Jane Porter and Anna Maria Porter
lived in Bristol, and Maria died at Mont-
pelier near by. These notes indicate but a
tithe of what may be seen and studied and
enjoyed in and about Bristol, — the city to
which poor Chatterton left his curse; the
region hallowed by the dust of Arthur
Hallam — the inspiration of Tennyson's
In Memoriam, the loftiest poem that has
been created in the English language since
the pen that wrote *Childe Harold* fell from
the divine hand of Byron.

VI.

THE LAND OF WORDSWORTH.

A GOOD way by which to enter the Lake District of England is to travel to Penrith and thence to drive along the shore of Ullswater, or sail upon its crystal bosom, to the blooming solitude of Patterdale. Penrith lies at the eastern slope of the mountains of Westmoreland, and you may there see the ruins of Penrith Castle, once the property and the abode of Richard, Duke of Gloucester, before he became King of England. Penrith Castle was one of the estates that were forfeited by the great Earl of Warwick, and King Edward IV. gave it to his brother Richard in 1471. Not much remains of this ancient structure, and the remnant is now occupied by a florist. I saw it, as I saw almost everything else in Great Britain during the summer of 1888, under a tempest of rain ; for it rained there, with a continuity almost ruinous, from the time of the lilac and apple-blossom till when the clematis began to show the splendour of its purple shield and the acacia to drop its milky blossoms on the autumnal grass. But travellers must not heed the weather. If there are dark days there are also bright ones — and one bright day in such a paradise as the English Lakes atones for the dreariness of a month of rain. Beside, even the darkest days may be brightened by gentle companionship. Henry Irving and Ernest Bendall, two of the most intellectual and genial men in England, were my associates in that expedition. We went from London into Westmoreland on a mild, sweet day in July, and we rambled for several days in that enchanted region. It was a delicious experience; and I often close my eyes and dream of it — as I am dreaming now.

In the drive between Penrith and Patterdale you see many things that are worthy of regard. Among these are the parish church of Penrith, a building made of red stone, remarkable for a massive square tower of great age and formidable aspect. In the adjacent churchyard are "The Giant's Grave" and "The Giant's Thumb," relics of a distant past that strongly and strangely affect the imagination. The grave is said to be that of Owen Cæsarius, a gigantic individual who reigned over Cumberland in remote Saxon times. The Thumb is a rough stone, about seven feet high, presenting a clumsy cross, and doubtless commemorative of another mighty warrior. Sir Walter Scott, who traversed Penrith on his journeys between Edinburgh and London, seldom omitted to pause for a view of those singular memorials — and Scott, like Wordsworth, has left upon this region the abiding impress of his splendid genius. " Ulfo's Lake " is Scott's name for Ullswater, and thereabout is laid the scene of his poem of *The Bridal of Triermain*. In Scott's day the traveller went by coach or on horseback, but now, "On lonely Threlkeld's solemn waste," at the foot of craggy Blencathara, you pause at a railway station having "Threlkeld" in large letters on its official signboard. Another strange thing that is passed on the road between Penrith and Patterdale is "Arthur's Round Table" — a circle of turf slightly raised above the surrounding level, and certainly remarkable, whatever may be its historic or antiquarian merit, for fine texture, symmetrical form, and lovely, luxuriant colour. Scholars think it was used for tournaments in the days of chivalry, but no one rightly knows anything about it, save that it is old. Not far from this bit of mysterious antiquity the road winds through a quaint village called Tirril, where, in the Quaker burial-ground, is the grave of an unfortunate young man, Charles Gough, who lost his life by falling from the Striding Edge of Helvellyn in 1805, and whose memory is hallowed by Wordsworth and Scott, in poems that almost every schoolboy has read, and could never forget — associated as they are with the story of the faithful dog for three months in that lonesome wilderness vigilant beside the dead body of his master,

> "A lofty precipice in front,
> A silent tarn below."

Patterdale possesses this advantage over certain other towns and hamlets of the lake region — that it is not much frequented by tourists. The coach does indeed roll through it at intervals, laden with those miscellaneous, desultory visitors whose pleasure it is to rush wildly over the land. And those objects serve to remind you that now, even as in Wordsworth's time, and in a double sense, "the world is too much with us." But an old-fashioned inn (Kidd's hotel) still exists at the head of Ullswater, to which fashion has not resorted and where kindness presides over the traveller's comfort. Close by also is a sweet nook called Glenridding, where, if you are a lover of solitude and peace, you may find an ideal abode. One house wherein lodging may be obtained was literally embowered in roses on that summer evening when first I strolled by the fragrant hay-fields on the Patterdale shore of Ullswater. The rose flourishes in wonderful luxuriance and profusion throughout Westmoreland and Cumberland. As you drive along the lonely roads your way will sometimes be, for many miles, between hedges that are bespangled with wild roses and with the silver globes of the laurel blossom, while all around you the lonely mountains, bare of foliage save for matted grass and a dense growth of low ferns, tower to meet the clouds. It is a wild place, and yet there is a pervading spirit of refinement over it all — as if Nature had here wrought her wonders in the mood of the finest art. And at the same time it is a place of infinite variety. The whole territory occupied by the lakes and mountains of this famous district is not more than fifty miles square; yet within this limit, comparatively narrow, are comprised all possible beauties of land and water that the most passionate devotee of natural loveliness could desire.

My first night in Patterdale was one of such tempest as sometimes rages in America about the time of the fall equinox. The wind shook the building. It was long after midnight when I went to rest, and the storm seemed to increase in fury as the night wore on. Torrents of rain were dashed against the windows. Great trees near by creaked and groaned beneath the strength of the gale. The cold was so severe that blankets were welcome. It was my first night in Wordsworth's country, and I thought of Wordsworth's lines: —

"There was a roaring in the wind all night;
The rain came heavily and fell in floods."

The next morning was sweet with sunshine and gay with birds and flowers, and all semblance of storm and trouble seemed banished forever.

"But now the sun is shining calm and bright,
And birds are singing in the distant woods."

Wordsworth's poetry expresses the inmost soul of those lovely lakes and mighty hills, and no writer can hope to tread, save remotely and with reverent humility, in the footsteps of that magician. You understand Wordsworth better, however, and you love him more dearly, for having rambled over his consecrated ground. There was not a day when I did not, in some shape or another, meet with his presence. Whenever I was alone his influence came upon me as something unspeakably majestic and solemn. Once, on a Sunday afternoon, I climbed to the topmost height of Place Fell (which is 2154 feet above the sea-level, while Scawfell Pike is 3210, and Helvellyn is 3118), and there, in the short space of two hours, I was thrice cut off by rain-storms from all view of the world beneath. Not a tree could I find on that mountain-top, nor any place of shelter from the blast and the rain — except when crouching beside the mound of rock at its summit, which in that country they call a "man." Not a living creature was visible, save now and then a lonely sheep, who stared at me for a moment and then scurried away. But when the skies cleared and the cloudy squadrons of the storm went careering over Helvellyn, I looked down into no less than fifteen valleys beautifully coloured by the foliage and the patches of cultivated land, each vale being sparsely fringed with little gray stone dwellings that seemed no more than card-houses, in those appalling depths. You think of Wordsworth in such a place as that—if you know his poetry. You cannot choose but think of him.

"Who comes not hither ne'er shall know
How beautiful the world below."

Yet somehow it happened that whenever friends joined in those rambles the great poet was sure to dawn upon us in a comic way. When we were resting on the bridge at the foot of "Brothers Water," which is a little lake, scarcely more than a mountain tarn, lying between Ullswater and the Kirkstone Pass, some one recalled that Wordsworth had once rested there and written a poem about it. We were not all as devout admirers of the bard as I am, and certainly it is not every one of the great author's compositions that a lover of his genius would wish to hear quoted under such circumstances. The Brothers Water poem is the one that begins "The cock is crowing, the stream is flowing," and I do not think that its insipidity is much relieved by its famous picture of the grazing cattle, "forty feeding like one." Henry Irving, not much given to enthusiasm about Wordsworth, heard those lines with undisguised merriment, and made a capital travesty of them on the spot. It is significant to remember, with reference to the inequality of Wordsworth, that on the day before he wrote "The cock is crowing," and at a place but a short distance from the Brothers Water bridge, he had written that peerless lyric about the daffodils — " I wandered lonely as a cloud." Gowbarrow Park is the scene of that poem — a place of ferns and hawthorns, notable for containing Lyulph's Tower, a romantic, ivy-clad lodge owned by the Duke of Norfolk, and Aira Force, a waterfall much finer than Lodore. Upon the lake shore in Gowbarrow Park you may still see the daffodils as Wordsworth saw them, a golden host, "glittering and dancing in the breeze." No one but a true poet could have made that perfect lyric, with its delicious close : —

> " For oft, when on my couch I lie
>   In vacant or in pensive mood,
> They flash upon that inward eye
>   Which is the bliss of solitude:
> And then my heart with pleasure fills,
> And dances with the daffodils."

The third and fourth lines were written

by the poet's wife — and they show that she was not a poet's wife in vain. It must have been in his " vacant mood " that he rested and wrote on the bridge at Brothers Water. " I saw Wordsworth often when I was a child," Frank Marshall[1] said (who had joined us at Penrith); " he used to come to my father's house, Patterdale Hall, and once I was sent to the garden by Mrs. Wordsworth to call him to supper. He was musing there, I suppose. He had a long, horse-like face. I don't think I liked him. I said, ' Your wife wants you.' He looked down at me and he answered, ' My boy, you should say Mrs. Wordsworth, and not "your wife."' I looked up at him and I replied, ' She *is* your wife, isn't she?' Whereupon he said no more. I don't think he liked me either." We were going up Kirkstone Pass when Marshall told this story — which seemed to bring the pensive and homely poet plainly before us. An hour later at the top of the pass, while waiting in the old inn called the Travellers' Rest, which incorrectly proclaims it-

---

[1] F. A. Marshall, editor of *The Henry Irving edition of Shakespeare* and author of *A Study of Hamlet*, the comedy of *False Shame*, and many other works, died in London, December, 1889, much lamented.

self the highest inhabited house in England [it is 1481 feet above the sea-level, whereas the inn called The Cat and Fiddle, — a corruption of Caton le Fidèle, governor of Calais, — on Axe Edge, near Buxton, is 1700 feet above the level of the sea], I spoke with an ancient, weather-beaten hostler, not wholly unfamiliar with the medicinal virtue of ardent spirits, and asked for his opinion of the great lake poet. They all know him in that region. "Well," he said, "people are always talking about Wordsworth, but I don't see much in it. I've read it, but I don't care for it. It's dry stuff — it don't chime." Truly there are all sorts of views, just as there are all sorts of people.

Mementos of Wordsworth are frequently encountered by the traveller among these lakes and fells. One of these, situated at the foot of Place Fell, is a rustic cottage that the poet once selected for his residence, and partly purchased. It somewhat resembles the Shakespeare cottage at Stratford — the living-room being floored with stone slabs, irregular in size and shape and mostly broken by hard use. In a corner of the kitchen stands a fine carved oak cupboard, dark with age, inscribed with the date of the Merry Monarch, 1660.

What were the sights of those sweet days that linger still, and will always linger, in my remembrance? A ramble in the old park of Patterdale Hall, which is full of American trees; a golden morning in Dovedale, with Henry Irving, much like Jaques, reclined upon a shaded rock, half-way up the mountain, musing and moralising in his sweet, kind way, beside the brawling stream; the first prospect of Windermere, from above Ambleside — a vision of heaven upon earth; the drive by Rydal Water, which has all the loveliness of celestial pictures seen in dreams; the glimpse of stately Rydal Hall and of the sequestered Rydal Mount, where Wordsworth so long lived and where he died; the Wishing Gate, where one of us, I know, wished in his heart that he could be young again and be wiser than to waste his youth in self-willed folly; the restful hours of observation and thought at delicious Grasmere, where we stood in silence at Wordsworth's grave and heard the murmur of Rotha singing at his feet; the lovely drive past Matterdale, across the moorlands, with only clouds and rooks for our chance companions, and mountains for sentinels along our way; the ramble through Keswick, all golden and glowing in the afternoon sun, till we stood by Crosthwaite church and read the words of commemoration that grace the tomb of Robert Southey; the divine circuit of Derwent — surely the loveliest sheet of water in England; the descent into the vale of Keswick, with sunset on the rippling crystal of the lake and the perfume of countless wild roses on the evening wind. These things, and the midnight talk about these things — Irving, so tranquil, so gentle, so full of keen and sweet appreciation of them — Bendall, so bright and thoughtful — Marshall, so quaint and jolly, and so full of knowledge equally of nature and of books! — can never be forgotten. In one heart they are cherished forever.

Wordsworth is buried in Grasmere churchyard, close by the wall, on the bank of the little river Rotha. "Sing him thy best," said Matthew Arnold, in his lovely dirge for the great poet —

"Sing him thy best! for few or none
Hears thy voice right, now he is gone."

In the same grave with Wordsworth sleeps his devoted wife. Beside them rest the poet's no less devoted sister Dorothy (who died at Rydal Mount in 1855, aged

83), and his favourite daughter, Dora, together with her husband, Edward Quillinan, of whom Arnold wrote so tenderly: —

"Alive, we would have changed his lot,
We would not change it now."

On the low gravestone that marks the sepulchre of Wordsworth are written these words: "William Wordsworth, 1850. Mary Wordsworth, 1859." In the neighbouring church a marble tablet on the wall presents this inscription: —

"To the memory of William Wordsworth. A true poet and philosopher, who by the special gift and calling of Almighty God, whether he discoursed on man or nature, failed not to lift up the heart to holy things, tired not of maintaining the cause of the poor and simple, and so in perilous times was raised up to be a chief minister, not only of noblest poetry, but of high and sacred truth. The memorial is raised here by his friends and neighbours, in testimony of respect, affection, and gratitude. Anno MDCCCLI."

A few steps from this memorable group will bring you to the marble cross that marks the resting-place of Hartley Coleridge, son of the great author of *The Ancient Mariner*, himself a poet of exquisite genius; and close by is a touching memorial to the gifted man who inspired Matthew Arnold's poems of *The Scholar-Gipsy* and *Thyrsis*. This is a slab laid upon his mother's grave, at the foot of her own tombstone, inscribed with these words: —

"In memory of Arthur Hugh Clough, some time Fellow of Oriel College, Oxford, the beloved son of James Butler and Anne Clough. This remembrance in his own country is placed on his mother's grave by those to whom life was made happy by his presence and his love. He is buried in the Swiss cemetery at Florence, where he died, November 13, 1861, aged 42.

"'So, dearest, now thy brows are cold
I see thee what thou art, and know
Thy likeness to the wise below,
Thy kindred with the great of old.'"

Southey rests in Crosthwaite churchyard, about half a mile north of Keswick, where he died. They show you Greta Hall, a fine mansion on a little hill enclosed in tall trees, which for forty years, ending in 1843, was the poet's home. In the church is a marble figure of Southey, recumbent on a large stone sarcophagus, which does no justice to his great personal beauty. His grave is in the ground, a little way from the church, marked by a low flat tomb, on the end of which appears an inscription commemorative of an old servant who had lived fifty years in his family and is buried with him. There was a pretty scene at this grave. When I came near it Irving was already there, and was speaking to a little girl who had guided him to the spot. "If any one were to give you a shilling, my dear," he said, "what would you do with it?" The child was confused and she murmured softly, "I don't know, sir." "Well," he continued, "if any one were to give you two shillings, what would you do with it?" She said she would save it. "But what if it were three shillings?" he went on, and every time he spoke he dropped a silver coin into her hand, till he must have given her more than a dozen of them. "Four — five — six — seven — what would you do with the money?" "I would give it to my mother, sir," she answered at last, her little face all smiles, gazing up at the stately, sombre stranger, whose noble countenance never looked more radiant than it did then, with gentle kindness and pleasure. It is a trifle to mention, but it was touching in its simplicity; and that amused group around the grave of Southey, in the blaze of the golden sun of a July afternoon, with Skiddaw looming vast and majestic over all, will linger with me as long as anything lovely and of good report is treasured in my memory. Long after we had left the place I chanced to speak of its peculiar interest. "The most interesting thing I saw there," said Irving, "was that sweet child." I do not think the great actor was ever much impressed with the beauties of the lake poets.

Another picture glimmers across my dream — a picture of peace and happiness which may close this rambling reminiscence of gentle days. We had driven up the pass between Glencoin and Gowbarrow, and had reached Matterdale, on our way toward Troutbeck station — not the beautiful Windermere Troutbeck, but the less famous one. The road is lonely, but at Matterdale one sees a few houses, and there our gaze was attracted by a small gray church nestled in a hollow of the hillside. It stands sequestered in its little place of graves, with bright greensward around it and a few trees. A faint sound of organ music floated from this sacred building and seemed to deepen the hush of the summer wind and shed a holier calm upon the lovely solitude. We dismounted and softly entered the church. A youth and a maiden, apparently lovers, were sitting at the organ — the young fellow playing and the girl listening, and looking with tender trust and innocent affection into his face. He recognised our presence with a kindly nod, but went on with his anthem. I do not think she saw us at all. The place was full of soft, warm light streaming through the stained glass of Gothic windows and fragrant with perfume floating from the hayfields and the dew-drenched roses of many a neighbouring hedge. Not a word was spoken, and after a few moments we departed as silently as we had come. Those lovers will never know what eyes looked upon them that day, what hearts were comforted with the sight of their happiness, or how a careworn man, three thousand miles away, fanning upon his hearthstone the dying embers of hope, now thinks of them with tender sympathy, and murmurs a blessing on the gracious scene which their presence so much endeared.

VII.

SHAKESPEARE RELICS AT WORCESTER.

WORCESTER, July 23, 1889. — The present wanderer came lately to "the Faithful City," and these words are written in a midnight hour at the Unicorn Hotel. This place is redolent of the wars of the Stuarts, and the moment you enter it your mind is filled with the presence of Charles the Martyr, Charles the Merry, Prince Rupert, and Oliver Cromwell. From the top of Red Hill and the margin of Perry Wood — now sleeping in the starlight or momentarily vocal with the rustle of leaves and the note of half-awakened birds — Cromwell looked down over the ancient walled city which he had beleaguered. Upon the summit of the great tower of Worcester cathedral Charles and Rupert held their last council of war. Here was fought and lost (1651) the battle that made the merry monarch a hunted fugitive and an exile. With a stranger's interest I have rambled on those heights; traversed the battlefield; walked in every part of the cathedral; attended divine service there; revelled in the antiquities of Edgar Tower; roamed through most of the city streets; traced all that can be traced of the old wall — there is little remaining of it now, and no part that can be walked upon; explored the royal porcelain works, for which Worcester is rightly famous; viewed several of its old churches and its one theatre (in Angel street); entered its Guildhall, where they preserve a fine piece of artillery and nine suits of black armour that were left by Charles II. when he fled from Worcester; paced the dusty and empty Trinity Hall, now abandoned and condemned to demolition, where once Queen Elizabeth was feasted; and visited the old "Commandery" — a rare piece of antiquity, remaining from the tenth century — wherein the Duke of Hamilton died of his wounds, after Cromwell's "crowning mercy," and beneath the floor of which he was laid in a temporary grave. The Commandery is now owned and occupied by a printer of directories and guide-books (the genial and hospitable Mr. Littlebury), and there, as everywhere else in storied Worcester, the arts of peace prevail over all the scenes and all the traces of

> "Old, unhappy, far-off things
> And battles long ago."

In the Edgar Tower at Worcester they keep the original of the marriage-bond that was given as a preliminary to the marriage of William Shakespeare and Anne Hathaway, by Fulk Sandells and John Richardson, of Shottery. It is a long, narrow strip of parchment, and it has been glazed and framed. Two seals of light-coloured wax were originally attached to it, dependent by strings, but these were removed — apparently for the convenience of the mechanic who put this relic into its present frame. The handwriting is crabbed and obscure. There are but few persons who can read the handwriting in old documents of this kind, and thousands of such documents exist in the church-archives, and elsewhere in England, that have never been examined. The name of Hathaway in this marriage-bond resembles the name of Whateley. The contract vouches that there was no impediment, through consanguinity or otherwise, to the marriage of William Shakespeare and Anne Hathaway.

It was executed on November 28, 1582, and it is supposed that the marriage took place immediately — since the first child of it, Susanna Shakespeare, was baptized in the church of the Holy Trinity at Stratford on May 26, 1583. No registration of the marriage has been found, but that is no proof that it does not exist. The law in those days prescribed that the marriage-bond should designate three parishes within the residential diocese, in any one of which tne marriage might be made; but the custom in those days permitted the contracting parties, when they had complied with this legal requirement, to be married in whatever parish, within the diocese, they might prefer. Three parishes were named in the Shakespeare marriage-bond. The registers of two of them have been searched, and searched in vain. The register of the third — that of Luddington, which is close by Shottery — was destroyed long ago, in a fire that burnt down Luddington church; and conjecture therefore assumes that Shakespeare was married at Luddington. It may be so, but there is no certainty about it, and until every old church register in the ancient diocese of Worcester has been examined, the quest of the registration of his marriage ought not to be abandoned. Richard Savage, the learned and diligent librarian of the Shakespeare Birthplace, has long been occupied with this inquiry, and he has transcribed several of the old church registers in the vicinity of Stratford. The Rev. Thomas Proctor Wadley, another local antiquary of great learning and incessant industry, has also taken part in this labour. The long-desired entry of the marriage of William and Anne remains undiscovered, but one gratifying and valuable result of these investigations is the disclosure that many of the names used in Shakespeare's works are the names of persons who were residents of Warwickshire in his time. It has pleased various crazy sensation-mongers to ascribe the authorship of Shakespeare's writings to Francis Bacon. This could only be done by ignoring positive evidence — the evidence, namely, of Ben Jonson, who knew Shakespeare personally, and who has left a written description of the manner in which Shakespeare composed his plays. Effrontery was to be expected from the advocates of the preposterous Bacon theory ; but when they have ignored the positive evidence, and the internal evidence, and the circumstantial evidence, and every other sort of evidence, they have still a serious obstacle to surmount — an obstacle that the researches of such patient scholars as Mr. Savage and Mr. Wadley are strengthening day by day. The man who wrote Shakespeare's plays knew Warwickshire as it could only be known to a native of it; and there is no proof that Francis Bacon knew it or ever was in it.

With reference to the Shakespeare marriage-bond, and with reference to all the records that are kept in the Edgar Tower at Worcester, it should perhaps be said that they are not preserved with the scrupulous care to which such treasures are entitled. The Tower — a gray and venerable relic, an ancient gate of the monastery, dating back to the time of King John — affords an appropriate receptacle for those documents; but it would not withstand fire, and it does not contain either a fire-proof chamber or a safe. The Shakespeare marriage-bond — which assuredly ought to be in the Shakespeare Birthplace, at Stratford — was taken from the floor of a closet, where it had been lying, together with a number of dusty books, and I was kindly permitted to hold it in my hands and to examine it. The frame provided for this priceless relic is such as you may see on an ordinary school slate. From another dusty closet an attendant extricated a manuscript diary kept by William Lloyd, Bishop of Worcester (1627-1717), and by his man-servant, for several years, about the beginning of the reign of Queen Anne; and in this are many quaint and humorous entries, valuable to the student of history and manners. In still another closet, having the appearance of a rubbish-bin, I saw heaps upon heaps of old parchment and paper writings — a mass of antique registry that it would need the labour of several years to examine, decipher, and classify. Worcester is especially rich in old records, and it is not impossible that the missing clew to Shakespeare's marriage may yet be found on that spot — where nobody has expected to find it.

Worcester is rich also in a superb library, which, by the kindness of Mr. Hooper, the custodian, I was allowed to explore, high up beneath the roof of the lovely cathedral. That collection of books, numbering about five thousand, consists mostly of folios, many of which were printed in France. They keep it in a long, low, oak-timbered room, the triforium of the south aisle of the nave. The approach is by a circular stone staircase. In an anteroom to the library I saw a part of the ancient north door of this church, — a fragment dating back to the time of Bishop Wakefield, 1386 — to which is still affixed a piece of the skin of a human being. The tradition is that a Dane committed sacrilege, by stealing the sanctus bell from the high altar, and was thereupon flayed alive for his crime, and the skin of him was fastened to the cathedral door. In the library are magnificent editions of Aristotle and other classics; the works of the fathers of the church; a beautiful illuminated manuscript of Wickliffe's New Testament — written on vellum in 1381; and several books, in splendid preservation, from the press of Caxton and that of Wynken de Worde. The world moves — but printing is not better done now than it was then. This library, which is for the use of the clergy of the diocese of Worcester, was founded by Bishop Carpenter in 1461, and originally was stored in the chapel of the charnel-house.

Reverting to the subject of old documents, a useful word may perhaps be said here about the registers in Trinity church at Stratford — documents which, in a spirit of disparagement, have sometimes been designated as "copies." This sort of pertness in the discussion of Shakespearean subjects is not unnatural in days when fanatical zealots are allowed freely to besmirch the memory of Shakespeare, in their wildly foolish advocacy of what they call the Bacon theory of the authorship of Shakespeare's works. The facts about the Stratford Registers, as here set down, are stated, by one who has many times held them in his hands and explored their quaint pages. Those records are contained in twenty-two volumes. They begin with the first year of Queen Elizabeth, 1558, and they end, as to the old parchment form, in 1812. From 1558 to 1600 the entries were made in a paper book, of the quarto form, still occasionally to be found in ancient parish churches of England. In 1600 an order-in-council was made commanding that those entries should be copied into parchment volumes, for their better preservation. This was done. The parchment volumes, which have been freely shown to me by my good friend William Butcher, the parish clerk of Stratford, date back to 1600. The handwriting of the copied portion, covering the period from 1558 to 1600, is careful and uniform. Each page is certified, as to its accuracy, by the vicar and the churchwardens. After 1600 the handwritings vary. In the register of marriage a new handwriting appears on September 17 that year, and in the registers of Baptism and Burial it appears on September 20. The sequence of marriages is complete until 1756; that of baptisms and burials until 1812; when in each case a book of printed forms comes into use, and the expeditious march of the new age begins. The entry of Shakespeare's baptism, April 26, 1564, from which it is inferred that he was born on April 23, is extant as a certified copy from the earlier paper book. The entry of Shakespeare's burial is the original entry made in the original register.

Some time ago an American writer chose to declare that Shakespeare's widow — seven years his senior at the start, and therefore fifty-nine years old when he died — subsequently contracted another marriage. Mrs. Shakespeare survived her husband seven years, dying at the age of sixty-six. The entry in the Stratford register of burial contains, against the date of 1623, August 28, the names of "Mrs. Shakespeare" and "Anna uxor Richard James." These two names, written one above the other, are connected by a bracket on the left side; and this is supposed to be evidence that Shakespeare's widow married again. The use of the bracket could not possibly mislead anybody possessing the faculty of clear vision. When two or more persons were baptized or buried on the same day the parish clerk, in making the requisite entry in the register, connected their names with a bracket. Three instances of this practice occur upon a single page of the register, in the same handwriting, close to the page that records the burial, on the same day, of Mrs. Shakespeare, widow, and Anna the wife of Richard James. But folly needs only a slender hook on which to hang itself.

Prince Arthur, eldest son of Henry VII., is buried in a beautiful chapel in Worcester cathedral. Bishop Gauden rests there, who wrote *Eikon Basilike*. The Duke of Hamilton was transferred there, from the Commandery. And in the Sacrarium stands the tomb of King John (obiit October 19, 1216, at Newark), in which, when it was opened, in 1797, the remains of that tyrant presented a ghastly spectacle.

VIII.

BYRON AND HUCKNALL-TORKARD.

ON a night in 1785, when Mrs. Siddons was acting at Edinburgh, the play being *The Fatal Marriage* and the character Isabella, a young lady of Aberdeenshire, Miss Catherine Gordon, of Gight, was among the audience. There is a point in that tragedy at which Isabella recognises her first husband, whom she had supposed to be dead, and in whose absence she had been married to another, and her consternation, grief, and rapture are sudden and excessive. Mrs. Siddons, at that point, always made a great effect. The words are, "O my Biron, my Biron!" On this night, at the moment when the wonderful actress sent forth her wailing, heart-piercing cry, as she uttered those words, Miss Gordon gave a frantic scream, fell into violent hysterics, and was borne out of the theatre, repeating "O my Biron, my Biron!" At the time of that incident she had not met the man by whom she was afterward wedded — the Hon. John Byron, whose wife she became about a year later. Their first-born and only child was George Gordon, afterward Lord Byron, the poet; and among the many aspects of his life which impress the thoughtful reader of that strange and melancholy story none is more striking than the dramatic aspect of it — so strangely prefigured in this event.

Censure of Byron, whether as a man or as a writer, may be considered to have spent its force. It is a hundred years (January 22, 1888), since he was born, and almost as many since he died. Everybody who wished to say a word against him has had ample opportunity for saying it, and there is evidence that this opportunity has not been neglected. The record was long ago made up. Everybody knows that Byron's conduct was sometimes deformed with frenzy and stained with vice. Everybody knows that Byron's writings are occasionally marred with profanity and licentiousness, and that they contain a quantity of crude verse. If he had never been married, or if, being married, his domestic life had not ended in disaster and scandal, his personal reputation would stand higher than it does at present, in the esteem of virtuous society. If about one-third of what he wrote had never been published, his reputation as a man of letters would stand higher than it now does in the esteem of the sternest judges of literary art. After an exhaustive discussion of the subject in every aspect of it, after every variety of hostile assault, and after praise sounded in every key of enthusiasm and in every language of the world, these truths remain. It is a pity that Byron was not a virtuous man and a good husband. It is a pity that he was not invariably a scrupulous literary artist, that he wrote so much, and that almost everything he wrote was published. But, when all this has been said, it remains a solid and immovable truth that Byron was a great poet and that he continues to be a great power in the literature and life of the world. Nobody who pretends to read anything omits to read *Childe Harold.*

To touch this complex and delicate subject in only a superficial manner it may not be amiss to say that the world is under obligation to Byron, if for nothing else, for the spectacle of a romantic, impressive, and instructive life. His agency in that spectacle no doubt was involuntary, but

all the same he presented it. He was a
great poet; a man of genius; his faculty of
expression was colossal, and his conduct
was absolutely genuine. No man in literature ever lived who lived himself more
fully. His assumptions of disguise only
made him more obvious and transparent.
He kept nothing back. His heart was laid
absolutely bare. We know even more
about him than we know about Dr. Johnson
— and still his personality endures the test
of our knowledge and remains unique,
romantic, fascinating, prolific of moral admonition, and infinitely pathetic. Byron
in poetry, like Edmund Kean in acting, is a
figure that completely fills the imagination,
profoundly stirs the heart, and never ceases
to impress and charm, even while it afflicts,
the sensitive mind. This consideration
alone, viewed apart from the obligation
that the world owes to the better part of
his writings, is vastly significant of the
great personal force that is inherent in the
name and memory of Byron.

It has been considered necessary to account for the sadness and gloom of Byron's
poetry by representing him to have been a
criminal afflicted with remorse for his many
and hideous crimes. His widow, appar-

ently a monomaniac, after long brooding over the remembrance of a calamitous married life — brief but unhappy, and terminated in separation — whispered against him, and against his half-sister, a vile and hideous charge; and this, to the disgrace of American literature, was subsequently brought forward by a distinguished female writer of America, much noted for her works of fiction and especially memorable for this one. The explanation of the mental distress exhibited in the poet's writings was thought to be effectually provided in that disclosure. But, as this revolting and inhuman story — desecrating graves, insulting a wonderful genius, and casting infamy upon the name of an affectionate, faithful, virtuous woman — fell to pieces the moment it was examined, the student of Byron's grief-stricken nature remained no wiser than before this figment of a diseased imagination had been divulged. Surely, however, it ought not to be considered mysterious that Byron's poetry is often sad. The best poetry of the best poets is touched with sadness. *Hamlet* has never been mistaken for a merry production. *Macbeth* and *King Lear* do not commonly produce laughter. Shelley and Keats sing as near to heaven's gate as anybody, and both of them are essentially sad. Scott was as brave, hopeful, and cheery as any poet that ever lived, and Scott's poetry is at its best in his dirges and his ballads of love and loss. The *Elegy* and *The Ancient Mariner* certainly are great poems, but neither of them is festive. Byron often wrote sadly because he was a man of a melancholy temperament, and because he deeply felt the pathos of mortal life, the awful mystery with which it is surrounded, the pain with which it is usually attended, the tragedy with which it commonly is accompanied, the frail tenure with which its loves and hopes are held, and the inexorable death with which it is continually environed and at last extinguished. And Byron was an unhappy man for the reason that, possessing every elemental natural quality in excess, his exquisite goodness was constantly outraged and tortured by his inordinate evil. The tempest, the clangour, and the agony of his writings are denotements of the struggle between good and evil that was perpetually afflicting his soul. Had he been the wicked man depicted by his detractors he would have lived a life of comfortable depravity and never would have written at all. Monsters do not suffer.

The true appreciation of Byron is not that of youth but that of manhood. Youth is captured by his pictorial and sentimental attributes. Youth beholds him as a nautical Adonis, standing lonely upon a barren cliff and gazing at a stormy sunset over the Ægean sea. Everybody knows that familiar picture — with the wide, open collar, the great eyes, the wild hair, and the ample neckcloth flowing in the breeze. It is pretty but it is not like the real man. If ever at any time he was that sentimental image he speedily outgrew that condition, just as those observers of him who truly understand Byron have long outgrown their juvenile sympathy with that frail and puny ideal of a great poet. Manhood perceives a different individual and is captured by a different attraction. It is only when the first extravagant and effusive enthusiasm has run its course, and perhaps ended in revulsion, that we come to know Byron for what he is really worth, and to feel the tremendous power of his genius. Sentimental folly has commemorated him in the margin of Hyde Park, as in the fancy of many a callow youth and green girl, with the statue of a pretty sailor-lad waiting for a spark from heaven, while a big Newfoundland dog dozes at his feet. It is a caricature. Byron was a man, and terribly in earnest; and it is only by earnest persons that his mind and works are understood. At this distance of time the scandals of a corrupt age, equally with the frailties of its most brilliant and most illustrious poetical genius, may well be left to rest in the oblivion of the grave. The generation that is living at the close of the nineteenth century will remember of Byron only that he was the uncompromising friend of liberty; that he did much to emancipate the human mind from every form of bigotry and tyranny; that he augmented, as no man had done since Dryden, the power and flexibility of the noble English tongue; and that he enriched literature with passages of poetry which, for sublimity, beauty, tenderness, and eloquence, have seldom been equalled and have never been excelled.

It was near the close of a fragrant, golden summer day (August 8, 1884) when, having driven out from Nottingham, I alighted in the market-place of the little town of Hucknall-Torkard, on a pilgrimage to the grave of Byron. The town is modern and commonplace in appearance — a little straggling collection of low brick dwellings, mostly occupied by colliers. On that day it appeared at its worst; for the widest part of its main street was filled with stalls, benches, wagons, and canvas-covered structures for the display of vegetables and other commodities, which were thus offered for sale; and it was thronged with rough, noisy, and dirty persons, intent on barter and traffic, and not indisposed to boisterous pranks and mirth, as they pushed and jostled each other among the crowded booths. This main street ends at the wall of the graveyard in which stands the little gray church where Byron was buried. There is an iron gate in the centre of the wall, and in order to reach this it was necessary to thread the mazes of the market-place, and to push aside the canvas flaps of a peddler's stall which had been placed close against it. Next to the churchyard wall is a little cottage,[1] with its bit of garden, devoted in this instance to potatoes; and there, while wait-

[1] Since this paper was written the buildings that flanked the church wall have been removed, the street in front of it has been widened into a square, and the church has been "restored" and considerably altered.

ing for the sexton, I fell into talk with an aged man, who said that he remembered, as an eye-witness, the funeral of Byron. "The oldest man he seemed that ever wore gray hairs." He stated that he was eighty-two and that his name was William Callandyne. Pointing to the church he indicated the place of the Byron vault. "I was the last man," he said, "that went down into it before he was buried there. I was a young fellow then, and curious to see what was going on. The place was full of skulls and bones. I wish you could see my son; he's a clever lad, only he ought to have more of the *suaviter in modo*." Thus with the garrulity of wandering age he prattled on; but his mind was clear and his memory tenacious and positive. There is a good prospect from the region of Hucknall-Torkard church, and pointing into the distance, when his mind had been brought back to the subject of Byron, my venerable acquaintance now described, with minute specification of road and lane — seeming to assume that the names and the turnings were familiar to his auditor — the route of the funeral train from Nottingham to the church. "There were eleven carriages," he said. "They didn't go to the Abbey" (meaning Newstead), "but came directly here. There were many people to look at them. I remember all about it, and I'm an old man — eighty-two. You're an Italian, I should say," he added. By this time the sexton had come and unlocked the gate, and parting from Mr. Callandyne we presently made our way into the church of St. James, locking the churchyard gate behind us to exclude rough and possibly mischievous followers. A strange and sad contrast, I thought, between this coarse and turbulent place, by a malign destiny ordained for the grave of Byron, and that peaceful, lovely, majestic church and precinct at Stratford-upon-Avon which enshrine the dust of Shakespeare!

The sexton of the church of St. James and the parish clerk of Hucknall-Torkard was Mr. John Brown, and a man of sympathetic intelligence, kind heart, and interesting character I found him to be — large, dark, stalwart, but gentle alike in manner and feeling, and considerate of his visitors. The pilgrim to the literary shrines of England does not always find the neighbouring inhabitants either sympathetic with his reverence or conscious of especial sanctity or interest appertaining to the relics which they possess; but honest and manly John Brown of Hucknall-Torkard understood both the hallowing charm of the place and the sentiment, not to say the profound emotion, of the traveller who now beheld for the first time the tomb of Byron. This church has been restored and altered since Byron was buried in it in 1824, yet in the main it retains its fundamental structure and its ancient peculiarities. The tower, a fine specimen of Norman architecture, strongly built, dark and grim, gives indication of great age. It is of a kind often met with in ancient English towns: you may see its brothers at York, Shrewsbury, Canterbury, Worcester, Warwick, and in many places sprinkled over the northern heights of London: but amid its tame surroundings in this little colliery settlement it looms with a peculiar frowning majesty, a certain bleak loneliness, both unique and impressive. The church is of the customary crucial form — a low stone structure, peak-roofed outside, but arched within, the roof being supported by four great pillars on either side of the centre aisle, and the ceiling being fashioned of heavy timbers forming almost a true arch above the nave. There are four large windows on each side of the church, and two on each side of the chancel, which is beneath a roof somewhat lower than that of the main building. Under the pavement of the chancel and back of the altar rail — at which it was my privilege to kneel while gazing upon this sacred spot — is the grave of Byron.[1] Nothing is written on the stone that covers his sepulchre except the simple name of BYRON, with the dates of his birth and death, in brass letters, surrounded by a wreath of leaves in brass, the gift of the King of Greece; and never did a name seem more stately or a place more hallowed. The dust of the poet reposes between that of his mother, on his right hand, and that of his Ada — "sole daughter of my house and heart" — on his left. The mother died on August 1, 1811; the daughter, who had by marriage become the Countess of Lovelace, in 1852. "I buried her with my own hands," said the sexton, John Brown, when, after a little time, he rejoined me at the altar rail. "I told them exactly where he was laid when they wanted to put that brass on the

---

[1] Revisiting this place on September 10, 1890 I found that the chancel has been lengthened, that the altar and the mural tablets have been moved backward from the Byron vault, and that the gravestone is now outside of the rail.

stone; I remembered it well, for I lowered the coffin of the Countess of Lovelace into this vault, and laid her by her father's side." And when presently we went into a little vestry he produced the Register of Burials and displayed the record of that interment in the following words: "1852. Died at 69 Cumberland Place, London. Buried December 3. Aged thirty-six. — Curtis Jackson." The Byrons were a short-lived race. The poet himself had just turned thirty-six; his mother was only forty-six when she passed away. This name of Curtis Jackson in the register was that of the rector or curate then incumbent but now departed. The register is a long narrow book made of parchment and full of various crabbed handwritings — a record similar to those which are so carefully treasured at the church of the Holy Trinity at Stratford; but it is more dilapidated.

Another relic shown by John Brown was a bit of embroidery, presenting the arms of the Byron family. It had been used at Byron's funeral, and thereafter was long kept in the church, though latterly with but little care. When the Rev. Curtis Jackson came there he beheld this frail memorial with pious disapprobation. "He told me," said the sexton, "to take it home and burn it. I did take it home, but I didn't burn it; and when the new rector came he heard of it and asked me to bring it back, and a lady gave the frame to put it in." Framed it is, and likely now to be always preserved in this interesting church; and earnestly do I wish that I could remember, in order that I might speak it with honour, the name of the clergyman who could thus rebuke bigotry, and welcome and treasure in his church that shred of silk which once rested on the coffin of Byron. Still another relic preserved by John Brown is a large piece of cardboard giving the inscription which is upon the coffin of the poet's mother, and which bore some part in the obsequies of that singular woman — a creature full of faults, but the parent of a mighty genius, and capable of inspiring deep love. On the night after Byron arrived at Newstead, whither he repaired from London on receiving news of her illness, only to find her dead, he was found sitting in the dark and sobbing beside the corse. "I had but one friend in the world," he said, "and she is gone." He was soon to publish *Childe Harold*, and to gain hosts of friends and have the world at his feet; but he spoke what he felt, and he spoke the truth, in that dark room on that desolate night. Thoughts of these things, and of many other strange passages and incidents in his brief, checkered, glorious, lamentable life, thronged into my mind as I stood there in presence of those relics and so near his dust, while the church grew dark and the silence seemed to deepen in the dusk of the gathering night.

They have for many years kept a book at the church of Hucknall-Torkard (the first one, an album given by Sir John Bowring, and containing the record of visitations from 1825 to 1834, was stolen in the latter year), in which the visitors write their names; but the catalogue of pilgrims during the last fifty years is not a long one. The votaries of Byron are far less numerous than those of Shakespeare. Custom has made the visit to Stratford "a property of easiness," and Shakespeare is a safe no less than a rightful object of worship. The visit to Hucknall-Torkard is neither so easy nor so agreeable, and it requires some courage to be a worshipper of Byron — and to own it. No day passes without bringing its visitor to the Shakespeare cottage and the Shakespeare tomb; many

days pass without bringing a stranger to
the church of St. James. On the capital of
a column near Byron's tomb I saw two
mouldering wreaths of laurel, which had
hung there for years; one brought by the
Bishop of Norwich, the other by the American poet Joaquin Miller. It was good to
see them, and especially to see them close
by the tablet of white marble which was
placed on that church wall to commemorate
the poet, and to be her witness in death,
by his loving and beloved sister Augusta
Mary Leigh — a name that is the synonym
of noble fidelity, a name that in our day
cruel detraction and hideous calumny have
done their worst to tarnish. That tablet
names him " The Author of Childe Harold's
Pilgrimage "; and if the conviction of
thoughtful men and women throughout the
world can be accepted as an authority, no
name in the long annals of English literature is more certain of immortality than the
name of Byron. People mention the poetry
of Spenser and Cowley and Dryden and
Cowper, but the poetry of Byron they read.
His reputation can afford the absence of all
memorial to him in Westminster Abbey
and it can endure the neglect and censure
of the precinct of Nottingham. That city

rejoices in a stately castle throned upon a rock, and persons who admire the Stuarts may exult in the recollection that there the standard of Charles I. was unfurled in his fatal war with the Parliament of England; but all that really hallows it for the stranger of to-day and for posterity is its association with the name of Byron. You will look in vain, however, for any adequate sign of his former association with that place. It is difficult even to find prints or photographs of the Byron localities in the shops of Nottingham. One dealer, from whom I bought all the Byron pictures that he possessed, was kind enough to explain the situation in one expressive sentence: "Much more ought to be done here as to Lord Byron's memory, that is the truth; but the fact is the first families of the county don't approve of him."

When we came again into the churchyard, with its many scattered graves and its quaint stones and crosses leaning every way and huddled in a strange kind of orderly confusion, the great dark tower stood out bold and solitary in the gloaming, and a chill wind of evening had begun to moan around its pinnacles, and through its mysterious belfry windows, and in the few trees near by, which gave forth a mournful whisper. It was hard to leave the place, and for a long time I stood near the chapel, just above the outer wall of the Byron vault. And there the sexton told me the story of the White Lady — pointing, as he spoke, to a cottage abutting on the churchyard, one window in which commands an easy view of the place of Byron's grave. "There she lived," he said, "and there she died, and there" (pointing to an unmarked grave near the pathway, about thirty feet from the Byron vault) "I buried her." It is impossible to give his words or to indicate his earnest manner. In brief, this lady, whose story no one knew, had taken up her residence in this cottage long subsequent to the burial of Byron, and had remained there until she died. She was pale, thin, handsome, and she wore white garments. Her face was often to be seen at that window, whether by night or day, and she seemed to be watching the tomb. Once, when masons were repairing the church wall, she was enabled to descend into that vault, and therefrom she obtained a skull, which she declared to be Byron's, and which she scraped, polished, and made perfectly white, and kept always beneath her pillow. It was her request, often made to the sexton, that she might be buried in the churchyard close to the wall of the poet's tomb. "When at last she died," said John Brown, "they brought that skull to me, and I buried it there in the ground. It was one of the loose skulls from the old vault. She thought it was Byron's, and it pleased her to think so. I might have laid her close to this wall. I don't know why I didn't."

In those words the sexton's story ended. It was only one more of the myriad hints of that romance which the life and poetry of Byron have so widely created and diffused. I glanced around for some relic of the place that might properly be taken away: there was neither an ivy leaf blooming upon the wall nor a flower growing in all that ground; but into a crevice of the rock, just above his tomb, the wind had at some time blown a little earth, and in this a few blades of grass were thinly rooted. These I gathered, and still possess, as a memento of an evening at Byron's grave.

NOTE ON THE MISSING REGISTER OF
HUCKNALL-TORKARD CHURCH.

The Album that was given to Hucknall-Torkard Church, in 1825, by Sir John Bowring, to be used as a register of the names of visitors to Byron's tomb, disappeared from that church some time after the year 1834, and it has not since been found. It is supposed to have been stolen. In 1834 its contents were printed,— from a manuscript copy of it, which had been obtained from the sexton,— in a book of selections from Byron's prose, edited by " J. M. L." These initials stand for the name of Joseph Munt Langford, who died in 1884. The dedication of the register is in the following words: " To the immortal and illustrious fame of LORD BYRON, the first poet of the age in which he lived, these tributes, weak and unworthy of him, but in themselves sincere, are inscribed with the deepest reverence.— July 1825." At that time no memorial of any kind had been placed in the church to mark the poet's sepulchre; a fact which prompted Sir John Bowring to begin his Album with twenty-eight lines of verse, of which these are the best: —

"A still, resistless influence,
  Unseen but felt, binds up the sense . . .
  And though the master hand is cold,
  And though the lyre it once controlled
  Rests mute in death, yet from the gloom
  Which dwells about this holy tomb

Silence breathes out more eloquent
Than epitaph or monument."

This register was used from 1825 till 1834. It contains eight hundred and fifteen names, with which are intertwined twenty-eight inscriptions in verse and thirty-six in prose. The first name is that of Count Pietro Gamba, who visited his friend's grave on January 31, 1825: but this must have been a reminiscent memorandum, as the book was not opened till the following July. The next entry was made by Byron's old servant, the date being September 23, 1825: " William Fletcher visited his ever-to-be-lamented Lord and Master's tomb." On September 21, 1828 the following singular record was written : " Joseph Carr, engraver, Hound's Gate, Nottingham, visited this place for the first time to witness the funeral of Lady Byron [mother of the much lamented late Lord Byron], August 9th, 1811, whose coffin-plate I engraved, and now I once more revisit the spot to drop a tear as a tribute of unfeigned respect to the mortal remains of that noble British bard. 'Tho' lost to sight, to memory dear.'" The next notable entry is that of September 3, 1829: "Lord Byron's sister, the Honourable Augusta Mary Leigh, visited this church." Under the date of January 8, 1832 are found the names of "M. Van Buren, Minister Plenipotentiary from the United States; Washington Irving; John Van Buren, New York, U.S.A., and J. Wildman." The latter, no doubt, was Colonel Wildman, the proprietor of Newstead Abbey, Byron's old home, now owned by Colonel Webb. On August 5, 1832 "Mr. Bunn (manager of Drury Lane theatre, honoured by the acquaintance of the illustrious poet) visited Lord Byron's tomb, with a party." Edward F. Flower and Selina Flower, of Stratford-upon-Avon, record their presence, on September 15, 1832 — the parents of Charles Edward Flower and Edgar Flower, of Stratford, the former being the founder of the Shakespeare Memorial. There are several eccentric tributes in the register, but the most of them are feeble. One of the better kind is this: —

"Not in that palace where the dead repose
In splendid holiness, where Time has spread
His sombre shadows, and a halo glows
Around the ashes of the mighty dead,
Life's weary pilgrim rests his aching head.
This is his resting-place, and save his own
No light, no glory round his grave is shed:

But memory journeys to his shrine alone
To mark how sound he sleeps, beneath yon
simple stone.

"Ah, say, art thou ambitious? thy young
breast —
Oh does it pant for honours? dost thou chase
The phantom Fame, in fairy colours drest,
Expecting all the while to win the race?
Oh, does the flush of youth adorn thy face
And dost thou deem it lasting? dost thou
crave
The hero's wreath, the poet's meed of
praise?
Learn that of this, these, all, not one can
save
From the chill hand of death. Behold
Childe Harold's grave!"

IX.

HISTORIC NOOKS AND CORNERS.

STRATFORD-UPON-AVON, August 20, 1889. — The traveller who hurries through Warwickshire — and American travellers mostly do hurry through it — appreciates but little the things that he sees and does not understand how much he loses. The customary course is to lodge at the Red Horse — which is one of the most comfortable houses in England — and thus to enjoy the associations that are connected with the visits of Washington Irving. His parlour, his bedroom (number 15), his armchair, his poker, and the sexton's clock, mentioned by him in the *Sketch Book*, are all to be seen — if your lightning-express conductor will give you time enough to see them. From the Red Horse you are taken in a carriage, when you ought to be allowed to proceed on foot, and the usual round includes the Shakespeare Birthplace ; the Grammar School and Guild chapel ; the remains of New Place; Trinity church and the Shakespeare graves in its chancel; Anne Hathaway's cottage at Shottery; and, perhaps, the Shakespeare Memorial library and theatre. These are impressive sights to the lover of Shakespeare; but when you have seen all these you have only begun to see the riches of Stratford-upon-Avon. It is only by living in the town, by making yourself familiar with it in all its moods, by viewing it in storm as well as in sunshine, by roaming through its quaint, deserted streets in the lonely hours of the night, by sailing up and down its beautiful Avon, by driving and walking in the green lanes that twine about it for many miles in every direction, by becoming in fact a part of its actual being, that you obtain a genuine knowledge of that delightful place. Familiarity, in this case, does not breed contempt. The worst you will ever learn of Stratford is that gossip thrives in it; that its intellect is, with due exception, narrow and sleepy; and that it is heavily ridden by the ecclesiastical establishment. You will never find anything that can detract from the impression of beauty and repose made upon your mind by the sweet retirement of its situation, by the majesty of its venerable monuments, and by the opulent, diversified splendours of its natural and historical environment. On the contrary, the more you know of those charms the more you will love the town, and the greater will be the benefit of high thought and spiritual exaltation that you will derive from your knowledge of it; and hence it is important that the American traveller should be counselled for his own sake to live a little while in Stratford instead of treating it as an incident of his journey.

The occasion of a garden party at the rectory of a clerical friend at Butler's Marston gave opportunity to see one of the many picturesque and happy homes with which this region abounds. The lawns there are ample and sumptuous. The dwelling and the church, which are close to each other, are bowered in great trees. From the terraces a lovely view may be obtained of the richly coloured and finely cultivated fields, stretching away toward Edgehill, which lies a little south-east from Stratford-upon-Avon about sixteen miles, and marks the beginning of the Vale of the Red Horse. In the churchyard are the gray, lichen-covered remains of one of those ancient crosses from the steps of which the monks preached in the early days of the church. Relics of this class are deeply interesting for what they suggest of the people and the life of earlier times. A perfect specimen of the ancient cross may be seen at Henley-in-Arden, a few miles north-west of Stratford, where it stands in mouldering majesty at the junction of two roads in the centre of the village — strangely inharmonious with the petty shops and numerous inns of which that long and straggling but characteristic and attractive settlement is composed. The tower of the church at Butler's Marston, a gray, grim structure, "four-square to opposition," was built in the eleventh century — a period of much ecclesiastical activity in the British islands. Within it I found a noble pulpit of carved oak, dark with age, of the time of James I. There are many commemorative stones in the church, on one of which appears this lovely couplet, addressed to the shade of a young girl: —

"Sleep, gentle soul, and wait thy Maker's will!
Then rise unchanged, and be an angel still."

The present village of Butler's Marston — a little group of cottages clustered upon the margin of a tiny stream and almost hidden in a wooded dell — is comparatively new; for it has arisen since the time of the Puritan civil war. The old village was swept away by the Roundheads when Essex and Hampden came down to fight King Charles at Edgehill in 1642. That fierce strife waged all along the country-side, and you may still perceive there, in the inequalities of the land, the sites on which houses formerly stood. It is a sweet and peaceful place now, smiling with flowers and musical with the rustle of the leaves of giant elms. The clergyman farms his own glebe, and he has expended more than a thousand pounds in the renovation of his manse. The church "living" is not worth much more than a hundred pounds a year, and when he leaves the dwelling, if he should ever leave it, he loses the value of all the improvements that he has made. This he mentioned with a contented smile. The place, in fact, is a little paradise, and as I looked across the green and golden fields, and saw the herds at rest and the wheat waving in sun and shadow, and thought of the simple life of the handful of people congregated here, the words of Gray came murmuring into my mind: —

"Far from the madding crowd's ignoble strife
Their sober wishes never learned to stray;
Along the cool, sequestered vale of life
They kept the noiseless tenor of their way."

"Unregarded age, in corners thrown." Was that fine line suggested to Shakespeare by the spectacle of the old almshouse of the Guild, which stood in his time, just as it stands now, close to the spot where he lived and died? New Place, Shakespeare's home, stood on the northeast corner of Chapel Street (a continuation of High Street) and Chapel Lane. The Guild chapel stands on the southeast corner of those streets, immediately opposite to what was once the poet's home. Southward from the chapel, and adjacent to it, extends the long, low, sombre building that contains the Free Grammar School and the almshouse, founded by Thomas Jolyffe in 1482, and refounded in 1553 by King Edward VI. In that grammar school there is reason to believe that Shakespeare was educated; at first by Walter Roche, afterward by Simon Hunt — who doubtless birched the little boys then, even as the headmaster does now; it being a cardinal principle with the British educator that learning, like other goods, should be delivered in the rear.

In that almshouse doubtless there were many forlorn inmates, even as there are at present — and Shakespeare must often have seen them. On visiting one of the bedesmen I found him moving slowly, with that mild, aimless, inert manner and that bleak aspect peculiar to such remnants of vanishing life, among the vegetable vines and the profuse and rambling flowers in the sunny garden behind the house; and presently I went into his humble room and sat by his fireside. The scene was the perfect fulfilment of Shakespeare's line. A stone floor. A low ceiling crossed with dusky beams. Walls that had been whitewashed long ago. A small iron kettle, with water in it, simmering over a few smouldering coals. A rough bed, in a corner. A little table, on which were three conch-shells ranged in a row. An old arm-chair, on which were a few coarse wads of horsehair as a cushion. A bench, whereon lay a torn, tattered, soiled copy of the prayer book of the church of England, beginning at the epiphany. This sumptuous place was lighted by a lattice of small leaded panes. And upon one of the walls hung a framed placard of worsted work, bearing the inscription, "Blessed be the Lord for His

Unspeakable Gift." The aged, infirm pensioner doddered about the room, and when he was asked what had become of his wife his dull eyes filled with tears and he said simply that she was dead. "So runs the world away." The summons surely cannot be unwelcome that calls such an old and lonely pilgrim as that to his rest in yonder churchyard and to his lost wife who is waiting for him.

Warwickshire is hallowed by shining names of persons illustrious in the annals of art. Drayton, Greene, and Heminge, who belong to the Shakespeare period, were born there. Walter Savage Landor was a native of Warwick — in which quaint and charming town you may see the house of his birth, duly marked, close by the gate of Warwick Castle. Croft, the composer, was born near Ettington, hard by Stratford: there is a tiny monument commemorative of him in the ruins of Ettington church, near the manor-house. And in our own day Warwickshire has enriched the world with George Eliot and Ellen Terry. But it is a chief characteristic of England that whichever way you turn in it your footsteps fall on haunted ground. Everyday life there is continually impressed by incidents of historic association. In an old church at Greenwich I asked that I might be directed to the tomb of General Wolfe. "He is buried just beneath where you are now standing," the custodian said. It was an elderly woman who showed the place, and she presently stated that when a girl she once entered the vault beneath that church and stood beside the coffin of General Wolfe and took a piece of laurel from it, and also took a piece of the red velvet pall from the coffin of the old Duchess of Bolton, close by. That Duchess was Lavinia Fenton, the first representative of Polly, in *The Beggars' Opera*, who died in 1760, aged fifty-two.[1] "Lord Clive," the dame added, "is buried in the same vault." An impressive thought, that the ashes of the man who established Britain's power in America should at last mingle with the ashes of the man who gave India to England!

[1] Dr. Joseph Wharton, in a letter to the poet Gay, described her as follows: "She was a very accomplished and most agreeable companion; had much wit, good strong sense, and a just taste in polite literature. Her person was agreeable and well made; though I think she could never be called a beauty. I have had the pleasure of being at table with her wheher conversation was much admired by the first characters of the age, particularly old Lord Bathurst and Lord Granville."

X.

SHAKESPEARE'S TOWN.

To traverse Stratford-upon-Avon is to return upon old tracks, but no matter how often you visit that delightful place you will always see new sights in it and find new incidents. After repeated visits to Shakespeare's town the traveller begins to take more notice than perhaps at first he did of its everyday life. In former days the observer had no eyes except for the Shakespeare shrines. The addition of a new wing to the ancient Red Horse, the new gardens around the Memorial theatre, the new chimes of Trinity — these, and matters like to these, attract attention now. And now, too, I have rambled, in the gloaming, through scented fields to Clifford church; and strolled through many a green lane to beautiful Preston and climbed Borden hill; and stood by the maypole on Welford common; and journeyed along the battle-haunted crest of

Edgehill; and rested at venerable Compton-Winyate; and climbed the hills of Welcombe to peer into the darkening valleys of the Avon and hear the cuckoo-note echoed and re-echoed from rhododendron groves, and from the great, mysterious elms that embower this country-side for miles and miles around. This is the life of Stratford to-day — the fertile farms, the garnished meadows, the avenues of white and coral hawthorn, masses of milky snow-ball, honeysuckle, and syringa loading the soft air with fragrance, chestnuts dropping blooms of pink and white, and laburnums swinging their golden censers in the breeze.

The building that forms the southeast corner of High Street and Bridge Street in Stratford was occupied in Shakespeare's time by Thomas Quiney, a wine-dealer who married the poet's youngest daughter, Judith, and an inscription appears upon it, stating that Judith lived in it for thirty-six years. Richard Savage, that competent, patient, diligent student of the church registers and other documentary treasures of Warwickshire, furnished the proof of this fact from investigation of the town records — which is but one of many services that he has rendered to the old home of Shake speare. The Quiney premises are now occupied by Edward Fox, a journalist, a printer, and a dealer in souvenirs of Shakespeare and of Stratford. This house, in old times, was officially styled The Cage, because it had been used as a prison. Standing in the cellar of it you perceive that its walls are four feet thick. There likewise are seen traces of the grooves down which the wine-casks were rolled in the days of Shakespeare's son-in-law, Thomas Quiney. The shop now owned by Edward Fox has been established in Stratford more than a hundred years, and as this tenant has a long lease of the building and is of an energetic spirit in his business it bids fair to last as much longer. One indication of his sagacity was revealed in the cellar, where was heaped a quantity of old oak, taken, in 1887, from the belfry of Trinity church, in which Shakespeare is buried. This oak, which was there when Shakespeare lived, and which had to be removed because a stronger structure was required for sustaining an augmented chime of heavy bells, will be converted into various carved relics, such as must find favour with Shakespeare worshippers — of whom more than sixteen thousand visited Stratford in 1887, at least one-

SHAKESPEARE'S TOWN. 145

fourth of that number, 4482, being Americans. A cross made of the belfry wood is a pleasing souvenir of the hallowed Shakespeare church. When the poet saw that church the tower was surmounted, not as now with a tall and graceful stone spire, but with a spire of timber covered with lead. This was removed and was replaced by the stone spire in 1763. The oak frame to support the bells, however, has been in the tower more than three hundred years.

The two sculptured groups, emblematic of Comedy and Tragedy, which have been placed upon the front of the Shakespeare Memorial theatre, are the gain of a benefit performance, given in that building on August 29, 1885, by Mary Anderson, who then, for the first time in her life, impersonated Shakespeare's Rosalind. That actress, after her first visit to Stratford — a private visit made in 1883 — manifested a deep interest in the town, and in consequence of her services to the Shakespeare Memorial she is now one of its life-governors. Those services completed the exterior decorations of the building. The emblem of History had already been put in its place — the scene in *King John* in which Prince Arthur melts the cruel purpose of Hubert to burn out his

K

eyes. Tragedy is represented by Hamlet and the Gravedigger in their colloquy over Yorick's skull. In the emblem of Comedy the figure of Rosalind is that of Mary Anderson, in a boy's dress — a figure that may be deemed inadequate to the original but one that certainly is expressive of the ingenuous demeanour and artless grace of that gentle lady. The grounds south of the Memorial are diversified and adorned with lawns, trees, flowers, and commodious pathways, and that lovely, park-like enclosure — thus beautified through the liberality of Charles Edward Flower, the original promoter of the Memorial — is now free to the people, "to walk abroad and recreate themselves" beside the Avon. The picture gallery of the Memorial lacks many things that are needed, and it contains several things that it should lack. The library continues to grow, but the American department of it needs accessions. Every American edition of Shakespeare ought to be there, and every book, of American origin, on a Shakespeare subject. It was at one time purposed to set up a special case, surmounted with the American emblem, for the reception of contributions from Americans. The library contained, in

March 1890, five thousand seven hundred and ninety volumes, in various languages. Of English editions of the complete works of Shakespeare it contains two hundred and nine. A Russian translation of Shakespeare, in nine volumes, appears in the collection, together with three complete editions in Dutch. An elaborate and beautiful catalogue of those treasures, made by Mr. Frederic Hawley, records them in an imperishable form. Mr. Hawley, long the librarian of the Memorial, died at Stratford on March 13, 1889, aged sixty-two, and was buried at Kensal Green, in London, his wish being to rest in that place. Mr. Hawley had been an actor, under the name of Haywell, and he was the author of more than one tragedy in blank verse. Mr. A. H. Wall, who succeeded him as librarian, is a learned man, an antiquary, and an excellent writer. To him the readers of the *Stratford-upon-Avon Herald* are indebted for many instructive articles — notably for those giving an account of the original Shakespeare quartos acquired for the Memorial Library at the sale of the literary property of J. O. Halliwell-Phillipps. Those quartos are the *Merchant of Venice*, the *Merry Wives of Windsor*, and a first edition of *Pericles*. A copy of *Roger of Faversham* was also bought, together with two of the plays of Aphra Behn. Charles Edward Flower purchased at that sale a copy of the first folio of Shakespeare, and all four of the Shakespeare Folios (1623, 1632, 1663, 1685) now stand side by side in his private library at Avonbank. Mr. Flower intimated the intention of giving them to the Memorial library. [His death, May 3, 1892, will not defeat that purpose.]

A large collection of old writings was found in a room of the Grammar School, adjacent to the Guild chapel, in 1887. About five thousand separate papers were discovered, the old commingled with the new; many of them indentures of apprenticeship; many of them receipts for money; no one of them especially important as bearing on the Shakespeare story. Several of them are in Latin. The earliest date is 1560 — four years before the poet was born. One document is a memorandum "presenting" a couple of the wives of Stratford for slander of certain other women, and quoting their bad language with startling fidelity. Another is a letter from a citizen of London, named Smart, establishing and endowing a free school in Stratford for teaching English — the writer quaintly remarking that schools for the teaching of Latin are numerous, while no school for teaching English exists, that he can discover. Those papers have been classified and arranged by Richard Savage, but nothing directly pertinent to Shakespeare has been found in them. I saw a deed that bore the "mark" of Joan, sister of Mary Arden, Shakespeare's mother, but this may not be a recent discovery. All those papers are written in that "cramped penmanship" which baffled Tony Lumpkin — and which baffles wiser people than he was. Richard Savage, however, is skilful in reading this crooked and queer caligraphy; and the materials and the duty of exploring them are in the right hands. When the researches and conclusions of that scholar are published they will augment the mass of evidence already extant — much of it well presented by J. O. Halliwell-Phillipps — that the writer of Shakespeare's plays [1] was a man familiar with the neighbourhood, the names, and the everyday life of Stratford-upon-Avon; a fact which is not without its

---

[1] A cogent paper on this subject, the learned and logical work of John Taylor, Esq., may be found in the London *Athenæum*, February 9, 1889.

admonitory suggestiveness to those credulous persons who incline to heed the ignorant and idle theories and conjectures of Mr. Ignatius Donnelly. That dense person visited Shakespeare's town in the summer of 1888, and surveyed the scenes that are usually viewed, and was entertained by the vicar, the Rev. George Arbuthnot; but he attracted no attention other than the contempt he deserves. "He did not address himself to me," said Miss Chataway, who was then at the Birthplace, as its custodian; "had he done so I should have informed him that, in Stratford, Bacon is all gammon." She was right. So it is. And not alone in Stratford, but wherever men and women have eyes to see and brains to understand.

The spot on which Shakespeare died ought surely to be deemed as sacred as the spot on which he was born: yet New Place is not as much visited as the Birthplace — perhaps because so little of it remains. Only five hundred and thirty-seven visitors went there during the year ending April 13, 1888. In repairing the custodian's house at New Place the crossed timbers in the one remaining fragment of the north wall of the original structure were found, beneath plaster. Those have been left uncovered and their dark lines add to the picturesque effect of the place. The aspect of the old house prior to 1742 is known but vaguely, if at all. Shakespeare bought it in 1597, when he was thirty-three years old, and he kept it till his death, nineteen years later. The street — Chapel lane — that separates it from the Guild chapel was narrower than it is now, and the house stood in a grassy enclosure, encircled by a wall, the entrance to the garden being at some distance eastward down the lane, toward the river. The chief rooms in New Place were lined with square, sunken panels of oak, which covered the walls from floor to roof and probably formed the ceilings. Some of those panels — obtained when the Rev. Francis Gastrell tore down that house in 1759 — may be seen in a parlour of the Falcon Hotel. There is nothing left of New Place but the old well in the cellar, the fragments of the foundation, the lintel, the armorial stone, and the fragment of wall that forms part of the custodian's house. That custodian, Mr. Bower Bulmer, a pleasant, appreciative man, always attentive and genial, died on January 17, 1888, and his widow succeeded him in office. Another conspicuous and interesting Stratford figure, well known, and for a long time, was John Marshall, the antiquary, who died on June 25, 1887. Mr. Marshall occupied the building next but one to the original New Place, on the north side,— the house once tenanted by Julius Shaw, one of the five witnesses to Shakespeare's will. Mr. Marshall sold Shakespeare souvenirs and quaint furniture. He had remarkable skill in carving and his mind was full of knowledge of Shakespeare antiquities and the traditional lore of Stratford. His kindness, his eccentric ways, his elaborate forms of speech, and his love and faculty for art commended him to the respect and sympathy of all who really knew him. He was a character — and in such a place as Stratford such quaint beings are appropriate and uncommonly delightful. He will long be kindly remembered, long missed from his accustomed round. He rests now in an unmarked grave in Trinity churchyard, close to the bank of the Avon — just in front of the stone that marks the sepulchre of Mary Pickering; by which token the future pilgrim may know the spot. Marshall was well known to me, and we had many a talk about the antiquities of the town. Among my relics there is a precious piece of wood bearing this inscription, written by him: "Old Oak from Shakespeare's Birth-place, taken out of the building when it was Restored in 1858 by Mr. William Holtom, the contractor for the restoration, who supplied it to John Marshall, carver, Stratford-on-Avon, and presented by him to W. Winter, August 27th, 1885, J. M." Another valued souvenir of this quaint person, given by his widow to Richard Savage, of the Birthplace — a fine carved goblet, made from the wood of the renowned mulberry-tree planted by the poet in the garden of New Place, and cut down by the Rev. Francis Gastrell in 1756 — came into my possession, as a birthday gift, on July 15, 1891.

At the Shakespeare Birthplace you will no longer meet with those gentle ladies — so quaint, so characteristic, so harmonious with the place — Miss Maria Chataway and Miss Caroline Chataway. The former of these was the official custodian of the cottage, and the latter assisted her in the work of its exposition. They retired from office in June 1889, after seventeen years of service, the former aged seventy-eight, the latter seventy-six; and now — being infirm, and incapable of the active, incessant labour that was required of them by the multitude of visitors — they dwell in a little house in the Warwick Road, where their friends are welcomed, and where venerable and honoured age will henceforth haunt the chimney-corner, and "keep the flame from wasting by repose."[1] The new guardian of the Shakespeare Cottage is Joseph Skipsey,[2] of Newcastle, the miner poet: for Mr. Skipsey was trained in the mines of Northumberland, was long a labourer in them, and his muse sings in the simple accents of nature. He is the author of an essay on Burns, and of various other essays and miscellaneous writings. An edition of his poems, under the title of *Carols, Songs and Ballads* has been published in London, by Walter Scott, and that book will be found interesting by those who enjoy the study of original character and of a rhythmical expression that does not savour of the poetical schools. Mr. Skipsey is an elderly man, with grizzled hair, a benevolent countenance, and a simple, cordial manner. He spoke to me, with much ani-

[1] Miss Maria Chataway died on January 31, 1891.

[2] Mr. Skipsey resigned his position in October 1891.

mation, about American poets, and especially about Richard Henry Stoddard, in whose rare and fine genius he manifested a deep, thoughtful, and gratifying interest. The visitor no longer hears that earnest, formal, characteristic recital, descriptive of the house, that was given daily and repeatedly for so many years by Miss Caroline Chataway, — that delightful allusion to "the mighty dome" that was the "fit place for the mighty brain." The Birthplace acquires new treasures from year to year — mainly in its library, which is kept in perfect order by Richard Savage, that ideal antiquarian, who even collects and retains the bits of the stone floor of the Shakespeare room that become detached by age. In that library is preserved the original manuscript of Wheler's History of Stratford, together with his own annotated and interleaved copy of the printed book, which is thus enriched with much new material relative to the antiquities of the storied town.

In the Washington Irving parlour of the Red Horse the American traveller will find objects that are specially calculated to please his fancy and to deepen his interest in the place. Among these are the chair in which Irving sat; the sexton's clock to which he refers in the *Sketch Book;* an autograph letter by him; another by Longfellow; a view of Irving's house of Sunnyside; and pictures of Junius Booth, Edwin Booth, the elder and the present Jefferson, Mary Anderson, Ada Rehan, Elliston, Farren, Salvini, Henry Irving, and Ellen Terry. To invest that valued room with an atmosphere at once literary and dramatic was the intention of its decorator, and this object has been attained. When Washington Irving visited Stratford and lodged at the Red Horse the "pretty chambermaid," to whom he alludes, in his gentle and genial account of that experience, was Sally Garner — then in fact a middle-aged woman and plain rather than pretty. The head waiter was William Webb. Both those persons lived to an advanced age. Sally Garner was retired, on a pension, by the late Mr. Gardner, former proprietor of the Red Horse, and she died at Tanworth and was buried there. Webb died at Stratford. He had been a waiter at the Red Horse for sixty years, and he was esteemed by all who knew him. His grave, in Stratford churchyard, remained unmarked, and it is one among the many that were levelled and obliterated in 1888, by order of the present vicar. A few of the older residents of the town might perhaps be able to indicate its situation; but, practically, that relic of the past is gone — and with it has vanished an element of valuable interest to the annual multitude of Shakespeare pilgrims upon whom the prosperity of Stratford is largely dependent, and for whom, if not for the inhabitants, every relic of its past should be perpetuated. This sentiment is not without its practical influence. Among other good results of it is the restoration of the ancient timber front and the quaint gables of the Shakespeare hotel, which, already hallowed by its association with Garrick and the Jubilee of September 7, 1769, has now become one of the most picturesque, attractive, and representative buildings in Stratford.

There is a resolute disposition among Stratford people to save and perpetuate everything that is associated, however remotely, with the name of Shakespeare. Mr. C. F. Loggin, a chemist in the High Street, possesses a lock and key that were affixed to one of the doors in New Place, and also a sundial that reposed upon a pedestal in New Place garden, presumably in Shakespeare's time. The lock is made of brass; the key of iron, with an ornamented handle, of graceful design, but broken. On the lock appears an inscription stating that it was " taken from New Place in the year 1759, and preserved by John Lord, Esq." The sundial is made of copper, and upon its surface are Roman numerals distributed around the outer edge of the circle that encloses its rays. The corners of the plate are broken, and one side of it is bent. This injury was done to it by thieves, who wrenched it from its setting, on a night in 1759, and were just making away with it when they were captured and deprived of their plunder. The sundial also bears an inscription, certifying that it was preserved by Mr. Lord. New Place garden was at one time owned by one of Mr. Loggin's relatives, and from that former owner those Shakespeare relics were derived. Shakespeare's hand may have touched that lock, and Shakespeare's eyes may have looked upon that dial — perhaps on the day when he made Jaques draw the immortal picture of Touchstone in the forest, moralising on the flight of time and the evanescence of earthly things. *As You Like It* was written in 1599.

Another remote relic of Shakespeare is the shape of the foundation of Bishopton church, which remains distinctly traced, by ridges of the velvet sod, in a green field a little to the northwest of Stratford, in the direction of Wilmcote — the birthplace of Shakespeare's mother, Mary Arden. The parish of Bishopton adjoins that of Shottery, and Bishopton is one of the three places mentioned in association with Shakespeare's marriage with Anne Hathaway. Many scholars, indeed, incline to think that the wedding occurred there. The church was demolished about eighty years ago. The house in Wilmcote, in which, as tradition declares, Mary Arden was born, is seen at the entrance to the village, and is conspicuous for its quaint dormer windows and for its mellow colours and impressive antiquity. Wilmcote is rougher in aspect than most of the villages of Warwickshire, and the country immediately around it is wild and bleak; but the hedges are full of wildflowers and are haunted by many birds; and the wide, green, lonesome fields, especially when you see them in the gloaming, possess that air of melancholy solitude — vague, dream-like, and poetic rather than sad — which always strongly sways the imaginative mind. Inside the Mary Arden Cottage I saw nothing remarkable except the massive old timbers. That house as well as the Anne Hathaway cottage at Shottery, will be purchased and added to "the Amalgamated Trusts of Shakespeare's Birthplace, the Museum, and New Place." The Anne Hathaway cottage is falling into decay; it needs care; and as an authentic relic of Shakespeare and a charming bit of rustic antiquity its preservation is important, as well to lovers of the poet, all the world over, as to the town of Stratford, which thrives by his renown. The beautiful Guild chapel also needs care. The hand of restoration should, indeed, touch it lightly and reverently; but restored it must be, at no distant day, for every autumn storm shakes down fragments of its fretted masonry and despoils the venerable grandeur of that gray tower on which Shakespeare so often gazed from the windows of his hallowed home. Whatever is done there, fortunately for the Shakespearean world, will be done under the direction of a man of noble spirit, rare ability, sound scholarship, and fine taste — the Rev. R. S. De Courcy Laffan, headmaster of the Grammar School and therefore pastor of the

Guild. Liberal in thought, manly in character, simple, sincere, and full of sensibility and goodness, that preacher strongly impresses all who approach him, and is one of the most imposing figures in the pulpit of his time. And he is a reverent Shakespearean.

A modern feature of Stratford, interesting to the Shakespeare pilgrim, is Lord Ronald Gower's statue of the poet, erected in October 1888, in the Memorial garden. That work is infelicitous in its site and not fortunate in all of its details, but in some particulars it is fine. It consists of a huge pedestal, on the top of which is the full-length bronze figure of Shakespeare, seated in a chair, while at the four corners of the base are bronze effigies of Hamlet, Lady Macbeth, Henry V., and Falstaff. Hamlet is the expression of a noble ideal. The face and figure are wasted with misery, yet full of thought and strength. The type of man thus embodied will at once be recognised — an imperial, powerful, tender, gracious, but darkly introspective nature, broken and subjugated by hopeless grief and by vain brooding over the mystery of life and death. Lady Macbeth is depicted in her sleep-walking, and, although the figure is treated in a conventional manner, it conveys the idea of remorse and of physical emaciation from suffering, and likewise the sense of being haunted and accursed. Prince Henry is represented as he may have appeared when putting on his dying father's kingly crown. The figure is lithe, graceful, and spirited; the pose is true and the action is natural; but the personality is deficient of identity and of royal distinction. Falstaff appears as a fat man who is a type of gross, chuckling humour; so that this image might stand for Gambrinus. The intellect and the predominant character of Falstaff are not indicated. The figures are dwarfed, furthermore, by the size of the stone that they surround — a huge pillar, upon which appropriate lines from Shakespeare have been inscribed. The statue of Shakespeare shows a man of solid self-concentration and adamantine will; an observer of universal view and incessant vigilance. The chief feature of it is the piercing look of the eyes. This is a man who sees, ponders, and records. Imagination and sensibility, on the other hand, are not suggested. The face lacks modelling: it is as smooth as the face of a child; there is not one characteristic curve or wrinkle in all its placid expanse. Perhaps it was designed to express an idea of eternal youth. The man who had gained Shakespeare's obvious experience must have risen to a composure not to be ruffled by anything that this world can do to bless or to ban a human life. But the record of his struggle must have been written in his face. This may be a fine statue of a practical thinker, but it is not the image of a poet and it is not an adequate presentment of Shakespeare. The structure stands on the south side of the Memorial building and within a few feet of it, so that it is almost swallowed up by what was intended for its background. It would show to better advantage if it were placed further to the south, looking down the long reach of the Avon toward Shakespeare's church. The form of the poet could then be seen from the spot on which he died, while his face would still look, as it does now, toward his tomb.

A constant stream of American visitors pours annually through the Red Horse. Within three days of July 1889 more than a hundred American names appeared in the register. The spirit of Washington Irving is mighty yet. Looking through a few of the old registers of this house, I came upon many familiar names of distinguished Americans. Bayard Taylor came here on July 23, 1856; James E. Murdoch (the famous Hamlet and Mirabel of other days) on August 31, 1856; Rev. Francis Vinton on June 10, 1857; Henry Ward Beecher on June 22, 1862; Elihu Burritt, "the learned blacksmith," on September 19, 1865; George Ripley on May 12, 1866. Poor Artemas Ward arrived on September 18, 1866 — only a little while before his death, which occurred in March 1867, at Southampton. The Rev. Charles T. Brooks, translator of *Faust*, registered his name here on September 20, 1866. Charles Dudley Warner came on May 6, 1868; Mr. and Mrs. W. J. Florence on May 29, 1868; and S. R. Gifford and Jervis M'Entee on the same day. The poet Longfellow, accompanied by Tom Appleton, arrived on June 23, 1868. Those Red Horse registers contain a unique and remarkable collection of autographs. Within a few pages, I observed the curiously contrasted signatures of Cardinal Wiseman, Sam Cowell, the Duc d'Aumale, Tom Thumb, Miss Burdett-Coutts (1861), Blanchard Jerrold, Edmund Yates, Charles Fechter, Andrew Carnegie,

David Gray (of Buffalo), the Duchess of Coburg, Moses H. Grinnell, Lord Leigh, of Stoneleigh Abbey, J. M. Bellew, Samuel Longfellow, Charles and Henry Webb (the Dromios), Edna Dean Proctor, Gerald Massey, Clarence A. Seward, Frederick Maccabe, M. D. Conway, the Prince of Condé, and John L. Toole. That this repository of autographs is appreciated may be inferred from the fact that special vigilance has to be exercised to prevent the hotel registers from being carried off or mutilated. The volume containing the signature of Washington Irving was stolen years ago and it has been vaguely heard of as being in America.

There is a collection of autographs of visitors to the Shakespeare Birthplace that was gathered many years since by Mary Hornby, custodian of that cottage (it was she who whitewashed the walls in order to obliterate the writings upon them, when she was removed from her office in 1820), and this is now in the possession of her granddaughter, Mrs. Smith, a resident in Stratford; but many valuable names have been taken from it — among others that of Lord Byron. The mania for obtaining relics of Stratford antiquity is remarkable. Mention is made of an unknown lady who came to the birth-room of Shakespeare, and, after begging in vain for a piece of the woodwork or of the stone, presently knelt and wiped the floor with her glove, which then she carefully rolled up and secreted, declaring that she would, at least, possess some of the dust of that sacred chamber. It is a creditable sentiment, though not altogether a rational one, that impels devotional persons to such conduct as that; but the entire Shakespeare cottage would soon disappear if such a passion for relics were practically gratified. The elemental feeling is one of reverence, and this is perhaps indicated in the following lines with which the present writer began a new volume of the Red Horse register, on July 21, 1889:—

Shakespeare.

While evening waits and hearkens,
  While yet the song-bird calls,—
Before the last light darkens,
  Before the last leaf falls,—
Once more with reverent feeling
  This sacred shrine I seek;
By silent awe revealing
  The love I cannot speak.

XI.

UP AND DOWN THE AVON.

STRATFORD-UPON-AVON, August 22, 1889. — The river life of Stratford is one of the chief delights of this delightful town. The Avon, according to law, is navigable from its mouth, at Tewkesbury, where it empties into the Severn, as far upward as Warwick; but according to fact it is passable only to the resolute navigator who can surmount obstacles. From Tewkesbury up to Evesham there is plain sailing. Above Evesham there are occasional barriers. At Stratford there is an abrupt pause at the Lucy mill, and your boat must be taken ashore, dragged a little way over the meadow, and launched again. The Lucy mill is just below the Shakespeare church, and from this point up to Clopton's bridge the river is broad. Here the boat-races are rowed almost every year. Here the stream ripples against the pleasure-ground called the Bancroft, skirts the gardens of the

Shakespeare Memorial, glides past the lovely lawns of Avonbank — the home of that noble public benefactor and fine Shakespearean scholar, Charles Edward Flower — and breaks upon the sustaining wall of the churchyard, crowned with the high and thick-leaved elms that nod and whisper over Shakespeare's dust. The town lies on the left or west bank of the Avon, as you ascend the river, looking northward. On the right or east bank there is a wide stretch of meadow. To float along here in the gloaming, when the bats are winging their "cloistered flight," when great flocks of starlings are flying rapidly over, when "the crow makes wing to the rooky wood," when the water is as smooth as a mirror of burnished steel, and equally the grasses and flowers upon the banks and the stately trees and the gray and solemn and beautiful church are reflected deep in the lucid stream, is an experience of thoughtful pleasure that sinks deep into the heart and will never be forgotten. You do not know Stratford till you know the Avon.

From Clopton's bridge upward the river winds capriciously between banks that are sometimes fringed with willows and sometimes bordered with grassy meadows or patches of woodland or cultivated lawns, enclosing villas that seem the chosen homes of all this world can give of loveliness and peace. The course is now entirely clear for several miles. Not till you pass the foot of Alveston village does any obstacle present itself; but there, as well as a little further on, by Hatton Rock, the stream runs shallow and the current becomes very swift, dashing over sandy banks and great masses of tangled grass and weeds. These are "the rapids," and through these the mariner must make his way by adroit steering and a vigorous and expert use of oars and boat-hooks. The Avon now is bowered by tall trees, and upon the height that it skirts you see the house of Ryon Hill — celebrated in the novel of *Asphodel*, by Miss Braddon. This part of the river, closed in from the world and presenting in each direction twinkling vistas of sun and shadow, is especially lovely. Here, in a quiet hour, the creatures that live along these shores will freely show themselves and their busy ways. The water-rat comes out of his hole and nibbles at the reeds or swims sturdily across the stream. The moor-hen flutters out of her nest among the long, green rushes and skims from bank to bank. The nimble little wagtail flashes through the foliage. The squirrel leaps among the boughs, and the rabbit scampers into the thicket. Sometimes a kingfisher, with his shining azure shield, pauses for a moment among the gnarled roots upon the brink. Sometimes a heron, disturbed in her nest, rises suddenly upon her great wings and soars grandly away. Once, rowing down this river at nearly midnight, I surprised an otter and heard the splash of his precipitate retreat. The ghost of an old gypsy, who died by suicide upon this wooded shore, is said to haunt the neighbouring crag; but this, like all other ghosts that ever I came near, eluded equally my vision and my desire. But it is a weird spot at night.

Near Alveston mill you must drag your boat over a narrow strip of land and launch her again for Charlecote. Now once more this delicious water-way is broad and fine as it sweeps past the stately, secluded homes upon the Warwick road. A great bed of cultivated white water-lilies (hitherto they have all been yellow) presently adorns it, and soon there are glimpses of the deer that browse or prance or slumber beneath the magnificent oaks and elms and limes and chestnuts of Charlecote Park. No view of

Charlecote can compare with the view of it that is obtained from the river; and if its proprietor values its reputation for beauty he ought to be glad that lovers of the beautiful sometimes have an opportunity to see it from this point. The older wing, with its oriel window and quaint belfry, is of a peculiar, mellow red, relieved against bright green ivy, to which only the brush of an artist could do justice. Nothing more delicious, in its way, is to be found; at least, the only piece of architecture in this region that excels it in beauty of colour is the ancient house of Compton-Winyate; but that is a marvel of loveliness, the gem of Warwickshire, and surpasses all its fellows. The towers of the main building of Charlecote are octagon, and a happy alternation of thin and slender with stout and stunted turrets much enhances the effect of quaintness in this grave and opulent edifice. A walled terrace, margined with urns and blazing with flowers of gold and crimson, extends from the river front to the water side, and terminates in a broad flight of stone steps, at the foot of which are moored the barges of the house of Lucy. No spectacle could suggest more of aristocratic state and austere magnificence than this sequestered edifice does, standing there, silent, antique, venerable, gorgeous, surrounded by its vast, thick-wooded park, and musing, as it has done for hundreds of years, on the silver Avon that murmurs at its base. Close by there is a lovely waterfall, over which some little tributary of the river descends in a fivefold wave of shimmering crystal, wafting a music that is heard in every chamber of the house and in all the fields and woodlands round about. It needs the sun to bring out the rich colours of Charlecote, but once when I saw it from the river a storm was coming on, and vast masses of black and smoke-coloured cloud were driving over it in shapeless blocks and jagged streamers, while countless frightened birds were whirling above it; and presently, when the fierce lightning flashed across the heavens and the deluge of rain descended and beat upon it, a more romantic sight was never seen.

Above Charlecote the Avon grows narrow for a space, and after you pass under Hampton Lucy bridge your boat is much entangled in river grass and much impeded by whirls and eddies of the shallowing stream. There is another mill at Hampton Lucy, and a little way beyond the village your further progress upward is stopped by a waterfall — beyond which, however, and accessible by the usual expedient of dragging the boat over the land, a noble reach of the river is disclosed, stretching away toward Warwick, where the wonderful Castle, and sweet St. Mary's tower, and Leicester's hospital, and the cosy Warwick Arms await your coming — with mouldering Kenilworth and majestic Stoneleigh Abbey reserved to lure you still further afield. But the scene around Hampton Lucy is not one to be quickly left. There the meadows are rich and green and fragrant. There the large trees give grateful shade and make sweet music in the summer wind. There, from the ruddy village, thin spires of blue smoke curl upward through the leaves and seem to tell of comfort and content beneath. At a little distance the gray tower of the noble church — an edifice of peculiar and distinctive majesty, and one well worthy of the exceptional beauty enshrined within it — rears itself among the elms. Close by the sleek and indolent cattle are crouched upon the cool sod, looking at you with large, soft, lustrous, indifferent eyes. The waterfall sings on, with its low and melancholy plaint, while sometimes the silver foam of it is caught up and whirled away by the breeze. The waves sparkle on the running stream, and the wild-flowers, in gay myriads, glance and glimmer on the velvet shore. And so, as the sun is setting and the rooks begin to fly homeward, you breathe the fragrant air from Scarbank and look upon a veritable place that Shakespeare may have had in mind when he wrote his line of endless melody —

"I know a bank where the wild thyme blows."

XII.

RAMBLES IN ARDEN.

STRATFORD-UPON-AVON, August 27, 1889.— Among the many charming rambles that may be enjoyed in the vicinity of Stratford, the ramble to Wootton-Wawen and Henley-in-Arden is not the least delightful. Both those places are on the Birmingham road; the former six miles, the latter eight miles from Stratford. When you stand upon the bridge at Wootton you are only one hundred miles from London, but you might be in a wilderness a thousand miles from any city, for in all the slumberous scene around you there is no hint of anything but solitude and peace. Close by a cataract tumbles over the rocks and fills the air with music. Not far distant rises the stately front of Wootton Hall, an old manor-house, surrounded with green lawns and bowered by majestic elms, which has always been a Catholic abode, and which is never leased to any but Catholic tenants.

A cosy, gabled house, standing among trees and shrubs a little way from the roadside, is the residence of the priest of this hamlet — an antiquarian and a scholar, of ample acquirements and fine talent. Across the meadows, in one direction, peers forth a fine specimen of the timbered cottage of ancient times — the black beams conspicuous upon the white surface of plaster. Among the trees, in another direction, appears the great gray tower of Wootton-Wawen church, a venerable relic and one in which, by means of the varying orders of its architecture, you may trace the whole ecclesiastical history of England. The approach to that church is through a green lane and a wicket-gate, and when you come near to it you find that it is surrounded with many graves, some marked and some unmarked, on all of which the long grass waves in rank luxuriance and whispers softly in the summer breeze. The place seems deserted. Not a human creature is anywhere visible, and the only sound that breaks the stillness of this August afternoon is the cawing of a few rooks in the lofty tops of the neighbouring elms. The actual life of all places, when you come to know it well, proves to be, for the most part, conventional, commonplace, and petty. Human beings, with here and there an exception, are dull and tedious, each resembling the other, and each needlessly laborious to increase that resemblance. In this respect all parts of the world are alike — and therefore the happiest traveller is he who keeps mostly alone, and uses his eyes, and communes with his own thoughts. The actual life of Wootton is, doubtless, much like that of other hamlets — a " noiseless tenor " of church squabbles, village gossip, and discontented grumbling, diversified with feeding and drinking, lawn tennis, matrimony, birth, and death. But as I looked around upon this group of nestling cottages, these broad meadows, green and cool in the shadow of the densely mantled trees, and this ancient church, gray and faded with antiquity, slowly crumbling to pieces amid the fresh and everlasting vitality of nature, I felt that surely here might at last be discovered a permanent haven of refuge from the incessant platitude and triviality of ordinary experience and the strife and din of the world.

Wootton-Wawen church is one of the numerous Catholic buildings of about the eleventh century that still survive in this realm, devoted now to Protestant worship. It has been partly restored, but most of it is in a state of decay, and if this be not soon arrested the building will become a ruin. Its present vicar, the Rev. Francis T. Bramston, is making vigorous efforts to interest the public in the preservation of this ancient monument, and those efforts ought to succeed. A more valuable ecclesiastical relic it would be difficult to find, even in this rich region of antique treasures, the heart of England. Its sequestered situation and its sweetly rural surroundings invest it with peculiar beauty. It is associated, furthermore, with names that are stately in English history and eminent and honoured in English literature — with Henry St. John, Viscount Bolingbroke, whose sister reposes in its ancient vaults, and with William Somerville, the poet who wrote *The Chase*. It was not until I actually stood upon his tombstone that my attention was directed to the name of that old author, and to the presence of his relics in this remote and lonely place. Somerville lived and died at Edston Hall, near Wootton-Wawen, and was famous in his day as a Warwickshire squire and huntsman. His grave is in the chancel of the church, and the following excellent epitaph, written by himself, is inscribed upon the plain blue stone that covers it: —

H. S. E.
OBIIT 17. JULY. 1742.
GULIELMUS SOMERVILE. ARM.
SI QUID IN ME BONI COMPERTUM HABEAS,
IMITATE.
SI QUID MALI, TOTIS VIRIBUS EVITA.
CHRISTO CONFIDE,
ET SCIAS TE QUOQUE FRAGILEM ESSE
ET MORTALEM.

Such words have a meaning that sinks deep into the heart when they are read upon the gravestone that covers the poet's dust. They came to me like a message from an old friend who had long been waiting for the opportunity of this solemn greeting and wise counsel. Another epitaph written by Somerville — and one that shows equally the kindness of his heart and the quaintness of his character — appears upon a little, low, lichen-covered stone in Wootton-Wawen churchyard, where it commemorates his huntsman and butler, Jacob

Bocter, who was hurt in the hunting-field, and died of this accident: —

H. S. E.
JACOBUS BOCTER.
GULIELMO SOMERVILE ARMIGRO
PROMUS ET CANIBUS VENATICIS
PRAEPOSITOR
DOMI. FORISQUE FIDELIS
EQUO INTER VENANDUM CORUENTE
ET INTESTINIS GRAVITER COLLISIS
POST TRIDUUM DEPLORANDUS.
OBIIT
28 DIE JAN.,
ANNO DNI 1719.
AETAT 38.

The pilgrim who rambles as far as Wootton-Wawen will surely stroll onward to Henley-in-Arden. The whole of that region was originally covered by the Forest of Arden[1] — the woods that Shakespeare had in mind when he was writing *As You Like It*, a comedy whereof the atmosphere, foliage, flowers, scenery, and spirit are purely those of his native Warwickshire. Henley,

---

[1] That learned antiquarian W. G. Fretton, Esq., of Coventry, has shown that the Forest of Arden covered a large tract of land extending many miles west and north of the bank of the Avon, around Stratford.

if the observer may judge by the numerous inns that fringe its long, straggling, picturesque street, must once have been a favourite halting-place for the coaches that plied between London and Birmingham. They are mostly disused now, and the little town sleeps in the sun and seems forgotten. There is a beautiful specimen of the ancient market-cross in its centre — gray and sombre and much frayed by the tooth of time. Close beside Henley, and accessible in a walk of a few minutes, is the church of Beaudesert, which is one of the most precious of the ecclesiastic gems of England. Here you will see architecture of mingled Saxon and Norman — the solid Norman buttress, the castellated tower, the Saxon arch moulded in zig-zag, which is more ancient than the dog-tooth, and the round, compact columns of the early English order. Above the church rises a noble hill, upon which, in the middle ages, stood a castle — probably that of Peter de Montfort — and from which a comprehensive and superb view may be obtained, over many miles of verdant meadow and bosky dell, interspersed with red-roofed villages from which the smoke of the cottage-chimneys curls up in thin blue spirals under the gray and golden sunset sky. An old graveyard encircles the church, and by its orderly disorder — the quaint, graceful work of capricious time — enhances the charm of its venerable and storied age. There are only one hundred and forty-six members of the parish of Beaudesert. I was privileged to speak with the aged rector, the Rev. John Anthony Pearson Linskill, and to view the church under his kindly guidance. In the ordinary course of nature it is unlikely that we shall ever meet again, but his goodness, his benevolent mind, and the charm of his artless talk will not be forgotten.[1] My walk that night took me miles away — to Claverdon and home by Bearley; and all the time it was my thought that the best moments of our lives are those in which we are touched, chastened, and ennobled by parting and by regret. Nothing is said so often as goodbye. But in the lovely words of Cowper —

"The path of sorrow, and that path alone,
Leads to the land where sorrow is unknown."

---

[1] This venerable clergyman died in the rectory of Beaudesert in February 1890 and was buried within the shadow of the church that he loved. The picturesque rectory of Beaudesert is the birthplace of Richard Jago [1715–1781], the poet who wrote *Edgehill*.

XIII.

THE STRATFORD FOUNTAIN.

AMERICAN interest in Stratford-upon-Avon springs out of a love for the works of Shakespeare as profound and passionate as that of the most sensitive and reverent of the poet's countrymen. It was the father of American literature — Washington Irving — who in modern times made the first pilgrimage to that holy land, and set the good example, which since has been followed by thousands, of worship at the shrine of Shakespeare. It was an American — the alert and expeditious P. T. Barnum — who by suddenly proposing to buy the Shakespeare cottage and transfer it to America startled the English into buying it for the nation. It is, in part, to American that Stratford owes the Shakespeare Memorial; for while the land on which it stands was given by that public-spirited citizen of Stratford, Charles Edward Flower — a sound and fine Shakespeare scholar, as his acting edition of the plays may testify — and while money to pay for the building of it was freely contributed by wealthy residents of Warwickshire, and by men of all ranks throughout the kingdom, the gifts and labours of Americans were not lacking to that good cause. Edwin Booth was one of the earliest contributors to the Memorial fund, and the names of Mr. Herman Vezin, Mr. M. D. Conway, Mr. W. H. Reynolds, Mrs. Bateman, and Mrs. Louise Chandler Moulton appear in the first list of its subscribers. Miss Kate Field worked for its advancement with remarkable energy and practical success. Mary Anderson acted for its benefit on August 29, 1885. In the church of the Holy Trinity, where Shakespeare's dust is buried, a beautiful stained window, illustrative, scripturally, of that solemn epitome of human life which the poet gives in the speech of Jaques on the seven ages of man, evinces the practical devotion of the American pilgrim; and many a heart has been thrilled with reverent joy to see the soft light that streams through its pictured panes fall gently on the poet's grave.

Wherever in Stratford you come upon anything that was ever associated, even remotely, with the name and fame of Shakespeare, there you will find the gracious tokens of American homage. The libraries of the Birthplace and of the Memorial alike contain gifts of American books. New Place and Anne Hathaway's Cottage are never omitted from the American traveller's round of visitations and duty of practical tribute. The Falcon, with its store of relics; the romantic Shakespeare Hotel, with its rambling passages, its quaint rooms named after Shakespeare's characters, its antique bar parlour, and the rich collection of autographs and pictures that has been made by Mrs. Justins; the Grammar School in which no doubt the poet, "with shining morning face" of boyhood, was once a pupil; John Marshall's antiquarian workshop, from which so many of the best souvenirs of Stratford have proceeded — a warm remembrance of his own quaintness, kindness, and originality being perhaps the most precious of them; the Town-Hall, adorned with Gainsborough's eloquent portrait of Garrick, to which no engraving does justice; the Guild chapel; the Clopton bridge; the old Lucy mill; the footpath across fields and roads to Shottery, bosomed in great elms; and the ancient picturesque building, four miles away, at Wilmcote, which was the home of Mary Arden, Shakespeare's mother, — each and every one of those storied places receives in turn the tribute of the wandering American, and each repays him a hundred-fold in charming suggestiveness of association, in high thought, and in the lasting impulse of sweet and soothing poetic reverie. At the Red Horse, where Mr. William Gardner Colbourne maintains the traditions of old-fashioned English hospitality, he finds his home; well pleased to muse and dream in Washington Irving's parlour, while the night deepens and the clock in the distant tower murmurs drowsily in its sleep. Those who will may mock at his enthusiasm. He would not feel it but for the spell that Shakespeare's genius has cast upon the world. He ought to be glad and grateful that he can feel that spell; and, since he does feel it, nothing could be more natural than his desire to signify that he too, though born far away from the old home of his race, and separated from it by three thousand miles of stormy ocean, has still his part in the divine legacy of Shakespeare, the treasure and the glory of the English tongue.

THE STRATFORD FOUNTAIN. 187

A noble token of this American sentiment, and a permanent object of interest to the pilgrim in Stratford, is supplied by the Jubilee gift of a drinking-fountain made to that city by George W. Childs of Philadelphia. It never is a surprise to hear of some new instance of that good man's constant activity and splendid generosity in good works; it is only an accustomed pleasure. With fine-art testimonials in the old world as well as at home his name will always be honourably associated. A few years ago he presented a superb window of stained glass to Westminster Abbey, to commemorate, in Poets' Corner, George Herbert and William Cowper. He has since given to St. Margaret's church, Westminster, where John Skelton and Sir James Harrington (1611-1677) were entombed, and where was buried the headless body of Sir Walter Raleigh, a pictorial window commemorative of John Milton. His fountain at Stratford was dedicated on October 17, 1887, with appropriate ceremonies conducted by the city's Mayor, Sir Arthur Hodgson of Clopton, and amid general rejoicing. Henry Irving, the leader of the English stage and the most illustrious of English actors since the age of Garrick, delivered an address, of singular felicity and eloquence, and also read a poem composed for the occasion by Oliver Wendell Holmes. The countrymen of Mr. Childs are not less interested in this structure than the community that it was intended to honour and benefit. They observe with satisfaction and pride that he has made this beneficent, beautiful, and opulent offering to a town which, for all of them, is hallowed by exalted associations, and for many of them is endeared by delightful memories. They sympathise also with the motive and feeling that prompted him to offer his gift as one among many memorials of the fiftieth year of the reign of Queen Victoria. It is not every man who knows how to give with grace, and the good deed is "done double" that is done at the right time. Stratford had long been in need of such a fountain as Mr. Childs has given, and therefore it satisfies a public want, at the same time that it serves a purpose of ornamentation and bespeaks and strengthens a bond of international sympathy. Rother Square, in which the structure stands, is the most considerable open tract in Stratford, and is situated near the centre of the town, on the west side. There, as also at the intersec-

THE STRATFORD FOUNTAIN. 189

tion of High and Bridge streets, which are the principal thoroughfares of the city, the farmers, at stated intervals, range their beasts and wagons and hold a market. It is easy to foresee that Rother, embellished with this monument, which combines a convenient clock-tower, a place of rest and refreshment for man, and commodious drinking-troughs for horses, cattle, dogs, and sheep, will soon become the agricultural centre of the region.

The base of the monument is made of Peterhead granite; the superstructure is of gray stone from Bolton, Yorkshire. The height of the tower is fifty feet. On the north side a stream of water flowing constantly from a bronze spout falls into a polished granite basin. On the south side a door opens into the interior. The decorations include sculptures of the arms of Great Britain alternated with the eagle and stripes of the American republic. In the second story of the tower, lighted by glazed arches, is placed a clock, and on the outward faces of the third story appear four dials. There are four turrets surrounding a central spire, each surmounted with a gilded vane. The inscriptions on the base are these: —

I.

The gift of an American citizen, George W. Childs, of Philadelphia, to the town of Shakespeare, in the Jubilee year of Queen Victoria.

II.

In her days every man shall eat, in safety
Under his own vine, what he plants; and sing
The merry songs of peace to all his neighbours.
God shall be truly known: and those about her
From her shall read the perfect ways of honour,
And by those claim their greatness, not by blood.
Henry VIII., Act v. Scene 4.

III.

Honest water, which ne'er left man i' the mire.
Timon of Athens, Act i. Scene 2.

IV.

Ten thousand honours and blessings on the bard who has thus gilded the dull realities of life with innocent illusions.—*Washington Irving's Stratford-on-Avon.*

Stratford-upon-Avon, fortunate in many things, is especially fortunate in being situated at a considerable distance from the main line of any railway. Two railroads indeed skirt the town, but both are branches, and travel upon them has not yet become too frequent. Stratford, therefore, still retains a measure of its ancient isolation, and consequently a flavour of quaintness. Antique customs are still prevalent there, and odd characters may still be encountered. The current of village gossip flows with incessant vigour, and nothing happens in the place that is not thoroughly discussed by its inhabitants. An event so important as the establishment of the American Fountain would excite great interest throughout Warwickshire. It would be pleasant to hear the talk of those old cronies who drift into the bar-parlour of the Red Horse on a Saturday evening, as they comment on the liberal American who has thus enriched and beautified their town. The Red Horse circle is but one of many in which the name of George W. Childs is spoken with esteem and cherished with affection. The present writer has made many visits to Stratford and has passed much time there, and he has observed on many occasions the admiration and gratitude of the Warwickshire people for the American philanthropist. In the library of

Charles Edward Flower, at Avonbank; in the opulent gardens of Edgar Flower, on the Hill; in the lovely home of Alderman Bird; at the hospitable table of Sir Arthur Hodgson, in Clopton house; and in many other representative places he has heard that name spoken, and always with delight and honour. Time will only deepen and widen the loving respect with which it is hallowed. In England more than anywhere else on earth the record of good deeds is made permanent, not alone with imperishable symbols, but in the hearts of the people. The inhabitants of Warwickshire, guarding and maintaining their Stratford Fountain, will not forget by whom it was given. Wherever you go, in the British islands, you find memorials of the past and of individuals who have done good deeds in their time, and you also find that those memorials are respected and preserved. Warwickshire abounds with them. Many such emblems might be indicated. Each one of them takes its place in the regard and gradually becomes entwined with the experience of the whole community. So it will be with the Childs Fountain at Stratford. The children trooping home from school will drink of it and sport

THE STRATFORD FOUNTAIN. 193

in its shadow, and, reading upon its base the name of its founder, will think with pleasure of a good man's gift. It stands in the track of travel between Banbury, Shipston, Stratford, and Birmingham, and many weary men and horses will pause beside it every day, for a moment of refreshment and rest. On festival days it will be hung with garlands, while all around it the air is glad with music. And often in the long, sweet gloaming of the summer times to come the rower on the limpid Avon, that murmurs by the ancient town of Shakespeare, will pause with suspended oar to hear its silver chimes. If the founder of that fountain had been capable of a selfish thought he could have taken no way better or more certain than this for the perpetuation of his name in the affectionate esteem of one of the loveliest places and one of the most sedate communities in the world.

Autumn in England — and all the country ways of lovely Warwickshire are strewn with fallen leaves. But the cool winds are sweet and bracing, the dark waters of the Avon, shimmering in mellow sunlight and frequent shadow, flow softly past the hallowed church, and the reaped and gleaned and empty meadows invite to many a healthful ramble far and wide over the country of Shakespeare. It is a good time to be there. Now will the robust pedestrian make his jaunt to Charlecote Park and Hampton Lucy, to Stoneleigh Abbey, to Warwick and Kenilworth, to Guy's Cliff, with its weird avenue of semi-blasted trees, to the Blacklow Hill — where sometimes at still midnight the shuddering peasant hears the ghostly funeral bell of Sir Piers Gaveston sounding ruefully from out the black and gloomy woods — and to many another historic haunt and high poetic shrine. All the country-side is full of storied resorts and cosy nooks and comfortable inns. But neither now nor hereafter will it be otherwise than grateful and touching to such an explorer of haunted Warwickshire to see, among the emblems of poetry and romance which are its chief glory, this new token of American sentiment and friendship, the Fountain of Stratford.

XIV.

BOSWORTH FIELD.

WARWICK, August 29, 1889. — It has long been the conviction of the present writer that the character of Richard III. has been distorted and maligned by the old historians from whose authority the accepted view of it is derived. He was, it is certain, a superb soldier, a wise statesman, a judicious legislator, a natural ruler of men, and a prince most accomplished in music and the fine arts and in the graces of social life. Some of the best laws that ever were enacted in England were enacted during his reign. His title to the throne of England was absolutely clear, as against the Earl of Richmond, and but for the treachery of some among his followers he would have prevailed in the contest upon Bosworth Field, and would have vindicated and maintained that title over all opposition. He lost the battle, and he was too great a man to survive the ruin of his fortunes. He threw away his life in the last mad charge upon Richmond that day, and when once the grave had closed over him, and his usurping cousin had seized the English crown, it naturally must have become the easy as well as the politic business of history to blacken his character. England was never ruled by a more severe monarch than the austere, crafty, avaricious Henry VII., and it is certain that no word in praise of his predecessor could have been publicly said in England during Henry's reign: neither would it have been safe for anybody to speak for Richard and the House of York in the time of Henry VIII., the cruel Mary, or the illustrious Elizabeth. The drift, in fact, was all the other way. The Life of Richard III. by Sir Thomas More is the fountain-head of the other narratives of his career, and there can be no doubt that More, who as a youth had lived at Canterbury, in the palace of Archbishop Morton, derived his views of Richard from that prelate — to whose hand indeed, the essential part of the Life has been attributed. "Morton is fled to Richmond." He was Bishop of Ely when he deserted the king, and Henry VII. rewarded him by making him

Archbishop of Canterbury. No man of the time was so little likely as Morton to take an unprejudiced view of Richard III. It is the Morton view that has become history. The world still looks at Richard through the eyes of his victorious foe. Moreover, the Morton view has been stamped indelibly upon the imagination and the credulity of mankind by the overwhelming and irresistible genius of Shakespeare — who wrote *Richard III.* in the reign of the granddaughter of Henry VII., and who, aside from the safeguard of discretion, saw dramatic possibilities in the man of dark passions and deeds that he could not have seen in a more human and a more virtuous monarch. Goodness is generally monotonous. "The low sun makes the colour." It is not to be supposed that Richard was a model man; but there are good reasons for thinking that he was not so black as his enemies painted him; and, good or bad, he is one of the most fascinating personalities that history and literature have made immortal. It was with no common emotion, therefore, that I stood upon the summit of Ambien Hill and looked downward over the plain where Richard fought his last fight and went gloriously to his death.

The battle of Bosworth Field was fought on August 22, 1485. More than four hundred years have passed since then: yet except for the incursions of a canal and a railway the aspect of that plain is but little changed from what it was when Richard surveyed it on that gray and sombre morning when he beheld the forces of Richmond advancing past the marsh and knew that the crisis of his life had come. The earl was pressing forward that day from Tamworth and Atherstone, which are in the northern part of Warwickshire — the latter being close upon the Leicestershire border. His course was a little to the southeast, and Richard's forces, facing northwesterly, confronted their enemies from the summit of a long and gently sloping hill that extends for several miles, about east and west, from Market Bosworth on the right, to the vicinity of Dadlington on the left. The king's position had been chosen with an excellent judgment that has more than once, in modern times, elicited the admiration of accomplished soldiers. His right wing, commanded by Lord Stanley, rested on Bosworth. His left was protected by a marsh, impassable to the foe. Sir William Stanley commanded the left and had his headquarters in Dadlington. Richard rode in the centre. Far to the right he saw the clustered houses and the graceful spire of Bosworth, and far to the left his glance rested on the little church of Dadlington. Below and in front of him all was open field, and all across that field waved the banners and sounded the trumpets of rebellion and defiance. It is easy to imagine the glowing emotions — the implacable resentment, the passionate fury, and the deadly purpose of slaughter and vengeance — with which the imperious and terrible monarch gazed on his approaching foes. They show, in a meadow, a little way over the crest of the hill, where it is marked and partly covered now by a pyramidal structure of gray stones, suitably inscribed with a few commemorative lines in Latin, a spring of water at which Richard paused to quench his thirst before he made that last desperate charge on Radmore heath, when at length he knew himself betrayed and abandoned, and felt that his only hope lay in killing the Earl of Richmond with his own hand. The fight at Bosworth was not a long one. Both the Stanleys deserted the king's standard early in the day. It was easy for them, posted as they were, to wheel their forces into the rear of the rebel army at the right and the left. Nothing then remained for Richard but to rush down upon the centre, where he saw the banner of Richmond — borne at that moment by Sir William Brandon — and to crush the treason at its head. It must have been a charge of tremendous impetuosity. It bore the fiery king a long way forward on the level plain. He struck down Brandon with his own hand. He plainly saw the Earl of Richmond, and came almost near enough to encounter him, when a score of swords were buried in his body, and, hacked almost into pieces, he fell beneath heaps of the slain. The place of his death is now the junction of three country roads, one leading northwest to Shenton, one southwest to Dadlington, and one bearing away easterly toward Bosworth. A little brook, called Sandy Ford, flows underneath the road, and there is a considerable coppice in the field at the junction. Upon the peaceful sign-board appear the names of Dadlington and Hinckley. Not more than five hundred feet distant to the eastward rises the embankment of a branch of the Midland Railway, from Nuneaton to Leicester; while at about the same distance to the westward rises the similar embankment of a canal. No monument has been erected to mark the spot where Richard III. was slain. They took up his mangled body, threw it across a horse, and carried it into the town of Leicester, and there it was buried, in the church of the Gray Friars — also the sepulchre of Cardinal Wolsey — now a ruin. The only commemorative mark upon the battlefield is the pyramid at the well, and that stands at a long distance from the place of the king's fall. I tried to picture the scene of his final charge and his frightful death as I stood there upon the hillside. Many little slate-coloured clouds were drifting across a pale blue sky. A cool summer breeze was sighing in the branches of the neighbouring trees. The bright green sod was all alive with the sparkling yellow of the colt's-foot and the soft red of the clover. Birds were whistling from the coppice near by, and overhead the air was flecked with innumerable black pinions of fugitive rooks and starlings. It did not seem possible that a sound of war or a deed of violence could ever have intruded to break the Sabbath stillness of that scene of peace.

The water of King Richard's Well is a

shallow pool, choked now with moss and weeds. The inscription, which was written by Dr. Samuel Parr, of Hatton, reads as follows : —

> AQVA. EX. HOC. PVTEO. HAVSTA
> SITIM. SEDAVIT
> RICHARDVS. TERTIVS. REX. ANGLIAE
> CVM HENRICO. COMITE DE RICHMONDIA
> ACERRIME. ATQVE. INGENTISSIME. PRAELIANS
> ET. VITA. PARITER. AC. SCEPTRO
> ANTE NOCTEM. CARITVRVS
> II KAL. SEP. A. D. M.C.C.C.C.LXXXV.

There are five churches in the immediate neighbourhood of Bosworth Field, all of which were in one way or another associated with that memorable battle. Ratcliffe Culey church has a low square tower and a short stone spire, and there is herbage growing upon its tower and its roof. It is a building of the fourteenth century, one mark of this period being its perpendicular stone font, an octagon in shape, and much frayed by time. In three arches of its chancel, on the south side, the sculpture shows tri-foliated forms of exceptional beauty. In the east window there are fragments of old glass, rich in colour and quaint and singular. The churchyard is full of odd gravestones, various in shape and irregular in position. An ugly slate-stone is much used in Leicestershire for monuments to the dead. Most of those stones record modern burials, the older graves being unmarked. The grass grows thick and dense all over the churchyard. Upon the church walls are several fine specimens of those mysterious ray and circle marks which have long been a puzzle to the archæological explorer. Such marks are usually found in the last bay but one, on the south side of the nave, toward the west end of the church. On Ratcliffe Culey church they consist of central points with radial lines, like a star, but these are not enclosed, as often happens, with circle lines. Various theories have been advanced by antiquarians to account for these designs. Probably these marks were cut upon the churches, by the pious monks of old, as emblems of eternity and of the Sun of Righteousness.

Shenton Hall (1629), long and still the seat of the Woollastons, stood directly in the path of the combatants at Bosworth Field, and the fury of the battle must have raged all around it. The Hall has been re-cased, and, except for its old gatehouse and semi-octagon bays, which are of the Tudor style, it presents a modern aspect. Its windows open toward Radmore Plain and Ambien Hill, the scene of the conflict between the Red Rose and the White. The church has been entirely rebuilt — a handsome edifice of crucial form, containing costly pews of old oak, together with interesting brasses and busts taken from the old church which it has replaced. The brasses commemorate Richard Coate and Joyce his wife, and Richard Everard and his wife, and are dated 1556, 1597, and 1616. The busts are of white marble, dated 1666, and are commemorative of William Woollaston and his wife, once lord and lady of the manor of Shenton. It was the rule, in building churches, that one end should face to the east and the other to the west, but you frequently find an old church that is set at a slightly different angle — that, namely, at which the sun arose on the birthday of the saint to whom the church was dedicated. The style of large east and west windows, with trefoil or other ornamentation in the heads of the arches, came into vogue about the time of Edward I.

Dadlington was Richard's extreme left on the day of the battle and Bosworth was his extreme right. These positions were intrusted to the Stanleys, both of whom betrayed their king. Sir William Stanley's headquarters were at Dadlington, and traces of the earthworks then thrown up there, by Richard's command, are still visible. Dadlington church has almost crumbled to pieces, and is to be restored. It is a little low structure, with a wooden tower, stuccoed walls and a tiled roof, and it stands in a graveyard full of scattered mounds and slate-stone monuments. It was built in Norman times, and although still used it has long been little better than a ruin. One of the bells in its tower is marked "Thomas Arnold fecit, 1763"— but this is comparatively a modern touch. The church contains two pointed arches, and across its roof are five massive oak beams almost black with age. The plaster ceiling has fallen, in several places, so that patches of laths are visible in the roof. The pews are square, box-like structures, made of oak and very old. The altar is a plain oak table, supported on carved legs, covered with a cloth. On the west wall appears a tablet inscribed "Thomas Eames, church-warden, 1773." Many human skeletons, arranged in regular tiers, were found in Dadlington churchyard, when a much-beloved clergyman, the Rev. Mr. Bourne, was buried, in 1881; and it is believed that those are remains of men who fell at Bosworth Field. The only inn at this lonely place bears the quaint name of "The Dog and Hedgehog."

The following queer epitaph appears upon a gravestone in Dadlington churchyard. It is Thomas Bolland, 1765, who thus expresses his mind, in mortuary reminiscence:—

" I lov'd my Honour'd Parents dear,
I lov'd my Wife's and Children dear,
And hope in Heaven to meet them there.
I lov'd my Brothers & Sisters too,
And hope I shall them in Heaven view.
I lov'd my Vncle's, Aunt's, & Cousin's too
And I pray God to give my children grace
 the same to do."

Stoke Golding church was built in the fourteenth century. It stands now, a gray and melancholy relic of other days, strange and forlorn yet august and stately, in a little brick village, the streets of which are paved, like those of a city, with blocks of stone. It is regarded as one of the best specimens extant of the decorated style of early English ecclesiastical architecture. It has a fine tower and spire, and it consists of nave, chantry, and south aisle. There is a perforated parapet on one side, but not on the other. The walls of the nave and the chancel are continuous. The pinnacles, though decayed, show that they must have been beautifully carved. One of the decorative pieces upon one of them is a rabbit with his ears laid back. Lichen and grass are growing on the tower and on the walls. The roof is of oak, the mouldings of the arches are exceptionally graceful, and the capitals of the five main columns present, in marked diversity, carvings of faces, flowers, and leaves. The tomb of the founder is on the north side, and the stone pavement is everywhere lettered with inscriptions of burial. There is a fine mural brass, bearing the name of Brokesley, 1633, and a superb "stocke chest," 1636; and there is a sculptured font, of exquisite symmetry. Some of the carving upon the oak roof is more grotesque than decorative — but this is true of most other carving to be found in ancient churches; such, for example, as you may see under the miserere seats in the chancel of Trinity at Stratford-upon-Avon. There was formerly some beautiful old stained glass in the east window of Stoke Golding church, but this has disappeared. A picturesque stone slab, set upon the church wall outside, arrests attention by its pleasing shape, its venerable aspect, and its decayed lettering; the date is 1684. Many persons slain at Bosworth Field were buried in Stoke Golding churchyard, and over their nameless graves the long grass is waving in indolent luxuriance and golden light. So Nature hides waste and forgets pain. Near to this village is Crown Hill, where the crown of England was taken from a hawthorn bush, whereon it had been cast in the frenzied confusion of defeat, after the battle of Bosworth was over and the star of King Richard had been quenched in death. Crown Hill is a green meadow now, without distinguishing feature, except that two large trees, each having a double trunk, are growing in the middle of it. Not distant from this historic spot stands Higham-on-the-Hill, where there is a fine church, remarkable for its Norman tower. From this village the view is magnificent — embracing all that section of Leicestershire which is thus haunted with memories of King Richard and of the carnage that marked the final conflict of the white and red roses.

XV.

THE HOME OF DR. JOHNSON.

LICHFIELD, STAFFORDSHIRE, July 31, 1890. — To a man of letters there is no name in the long annals of English literature more interesting and significant than the name of Samuel Johnson. It has been truly said that no other man was ever subjected to such a light as Boswell threw upon Johnson, and that few other men could have endured it so well. He was many things that are noble, but for all men of letters he is especially noble as the champion of literature. He vindicated the profession of letters. He lived by his pen, and he taught the great world, once for all, that it is honourable so to live. That lesson was needed in the England of his period; and from that period onward the literary vocation has steadily been held in higher esteem than it enjoyed up to that time. You will not be surprised that one of the humblest of his followers should linger for a while in the ancient town that is glorified by association with his illustrious name, or should wish to send a word of fealty and homage from the birthplace of Dr. Johnson.

Lichfield is a cluster of rather dingy streets and of red-brick and stucco buildings, lying in a vale a little northward from Birmingham, diversified by a couple of artificial lakes and glorified by one of the loveliest churches in Europe. Without its church the town would be nothing; with its church it is everything. Lichfield cathedral, although an ancient structure — dating back, indeed, to the early part of the twelfth century — has been so sorely battered first and last, and so considerably "restored," that it presents the aspect of a building almost modern. The denotements of antiquity, however, are not entirely absent from it, and altogether it is not less venerable than majestic. No one of the cathedrals of England presents a more beautiful façade. The multitudinous statues of saints and kings that are upon it create an impression of royal opulence. The carving upon the recesses of the great doorways on the north and west is of astonishing variety and loveliness. The massive doors of dark oak, fretted with ironwork of rare delicacy, are impressive and altogether are suitable for such an edifice. Seven of the large gothic windows in the chancel are filled with genuine old glass — not, indeed, the glass that they originally contained, for that was smashed by the Puritan fanatics, but a great quantity (no less than at least 340 pieces, each about twenty-two inches square) made in Germany in the early part of the sixteenth century when the art of staining glass was at its summit of skill. This treasure was given to the cathedral by a liberal friend, Sir Brooke Boothby, who had obtained it by purchase, in 1802, from the dissolved Abbey of Herckenrode. No such colour as that old glass presents can be seen in the glass that is manufactured now. It is imitated indeed, but it does not last. The subjects portrayed in those sumptuous windows are mostly scriptural, but the centre window on the north side of the chancel is devoted to portraits of noblemen, one of them being Errard de la Marck, who was enthroned Bishop of Liège in 1505, and who, toward the end of his stormy life, adopted the old Roman motto — comprehensive and final — which, a little garbled, appears in the glass beneath his heraldic arms : —

"Decipimus votis; et tempore fallimur;
  Et Mors deridet curas; anxia vita nihil."

The father of the illustrious Joseph Addison was Dean of this cathedral from 1688 to 1703, and his remains are buried in the ground, near the west door. The stately Latin epitaph was written by his son. This and several other epitaphs here attract the interested attention of literary students. A tablet on the north wall, in the porch, commemorates the courage and sagacity of Lady Mary Wortley Montagu, who introduced into England the practice of inoculation for the small-pox. Anna Seward, the poet, who died in 1809, aged sixty-six, and who was one of the friends of Dr. Johnson, was buried and is commemorated here, and the fact that she placed a tablet here in memory of her father is celebrated in sixteen eloquent and felicitous lines by Sir Walter Scott. The father was a canon of Lichfield, and died in 1790. The reader of Boswell will not fail to remark the epitaph on Gilbert Walmesley, once registrar of the ecclesiastical court of Lichfield, and one of Dr. Johnson's especial friends. Of Chappel Woodhouse it is significantly said, upon his memorial stone, that he was "lamented most by those who knew him best." Here one sees two of the best works of Chantrey — one called "The Sleeping Children," erected in 1817, in memory of the two young daughters of the Rev. William Robinson; the other a kneeling figure of Bishop Ryder, who died in 1836. The former was one of the earliest triumphs of Chantrey — an exquisite semblance of sleeping innocence and heavenly purity [1] — and the latter was his last. Near by is placed one of the most sumptuous monuments in England, a recumbent statue, done by the master-hand of Watts, the painter, presenting Bishop Lonsdale, who died in 1867. This figure, in which the modelling is very beautiful and expressive, rests upon a bed of marble and alabaster. In Chantrey's statue of Bishop Ryder, which seems no effigy but indeed the living man, there is marvellous perfection of drapery — the marble having the effect of flowing silk. Here also, in the south transept, is the urn of the Gastrells, formerly of Stratford-upon-Avon, to whom was due the destruction (1759) of the house of New Place in which

---

[1] Chantrey had seen the beautiful sculpture of little Penelope Boothby, in Ashbourne church, Derbyshire, made by Banks, and he may well have been inspired by the spectacle.

Shakespeare died. No mention of the Rev. Gastrell occurs in the epitaph, but copious eulogium is lavished on his widow, both in verse and prose, and she must indeed have been a good woman if the line is true which describes her as "A friend to want when each false friend withdrew." Her chief title to remembrance, however, like that of her husband, is an unhallowed association with one of the most sacred of literary shrines. In 1776 Johnson, accompanied by Boswell, visited Lichfield, and Boswell records that they dined with Mrs. Gastrell and her sister Mrs. Aston. The Rev. Mr. Gastrell was then dead. "I was not informed till afterward," says Boswell, "that Mrs. Gastrell's husband was the clergyman who, while he lived at Stratford-upon-Avon, with Gothic barbarity cut down Shakespeare's mulberry-tree, and as Dr. Johnson told me, did it to vex his neighbours. His lady, I have reason to believe, on the same authority, participated in the guilt of what the enthusiasts of our immortal bard deem almost a species of sacrilege." The destruction of the house followed close upon that of the tree, and to both their deaths the lady was doubtless accessary.

Upon the ledge of a casement on the east

side of the chancel, separated by the central lancet of a threefold window, stand the marble busts of Samuel Johnson and David Garrick. Side by side they went through life; side by side their ashes repose in the great abbey at Westminster; and side by side they are commemorated here. Both the busts were made by Westmacott, and obviously each is a portrait. The head of Johnson appears without his customary wig. The colossal individuality of the man plainly declares itself in form and pose, in every line of the eloquent face and in the superb dignity of the figure and the action. This work was based on a cast taken after death, and this undoubtedly is Johnson's self. The head is massive yet graceful, denoting a compact brain and great natural refinement of intellect. The brow is indicative of uncommon sweetness. The eyes are finely shaped. The nose is prominent, long, and slightly aquiline, with wide and sensitive nostrils. The mouth is large, and the lips are slightly parted, as if in speech. Prodigious perceptive faculties are shown in the sculpture of the forehead — a feature that is characteristic, in even a greater degree, of the bust of Garrick. The total expression of the countenance is benignant, yet troubled and rueful. It is a thoughtful and venerable face, and yet it is the passionate face of a man who has passed through many storms of self-conflict and been much ravaged by spiritual pain. The face of Garrick, on the contrary, is eager, animated, triumphant, happy, showing a nature of absolute simplicity, a sanguine temperament, and a mind that tempests may have ruffled but never convulsed. Garrick kept his "storm and stress" for his tragic performances; there was no particle of it in his personal experience. It was good to see those old friends thus associated in the beautiful church that they knew and loved in the sweet days when their friendship had just begun and their labours and their honours were all before them. I placed myself where, during the service, I could look upon both the busts at once; and presently, in the deathlike silence, after the last amen of evensong had died away, I could well believe that those familiar figures were kneeling beside me, as so often they must have knelt beneath this glorious and venerable roof: and for one worshipper at least the beams of the westering sun, that made a solemn splendour through the church, illumined visions no mortal eyes could see.

THE HOME OF DR. JOHNSON.

Beneath the bust of Johnson, upon a stone slab affixed to the wall, appears this inscription:—

The friends of SAMUEL JOHNSON, LL.D., a native of Lichfield, erected this monument as a tribute of respect to the memory of a man of extensive learning, a distinguished moral writer and a sincere Christian. He died the 13th of December 1784, aged 75 years.

A similar stone beneath the bust of Garrick is inscribed as follows:—

Eva Maria, relict of DAVID GARRICK, Esq., caused this monument to be erected to the memory of her beloved husband, who died the 20th of January 1779, aged 63 years. He had not only the amiable qualities of private life, but such astonishing dramatick talents as too well verified the observation of his friend: "His death eclipsed the gayety of nations and impoverished the publick stock of harmless pleasure."

This "observation" is the well-known eulogium of Johnson, who, however much he may have growled about Garrick, always loved him and deeply mourned for him. These memorials of an author and an actor are not rendered the more impressive by being surmounted, as at present they are, in Lichfield cathedral, with old battle-flags — commemorative souvenirs of the 80th Regiment, Staffordshire volunteers — honourable and interesting relics in their place, but inappropriate to the effigies of Johnson and Garrick.

The house in which Johnson was born stands at the corner of Market street and Breadmarket street, facing the little Market Place of Lichfield. It is an antiquated building, three stories in height, having a long, peaked roof. The lower story is recessed, so that the entrance is sheltered by a pent. Its two doors — for the structure now consists of two tenements — are approached by low stone steps, guarded by an iron rail. There are ten windows, five in each row, in the front of the upper stories. The pent-roof is supported by three sturdy pillars. The house has a front of stucco. A bill in one of the lower windows certifies that now this house is "To Let." Here old Michael Johnson kept his bookshop, in the days of good Queen Anne, and from this door young Samuel Johnson went forth to his school and his play. The whole various, pathetic, impressive story of his long, laborious, sturdy, beneficent life drifts through your mind as you stand at that threshold and conjure up the pictures of the past. Opposite to the house, and facing it, is the statue of Johnson presented to Lichfield in 1838 by James Thomas Low, then Chancellor of the diocese. On the sides of its massive pedestal are sculptures, showing first the boy, borne on his father's shoulders, listening to the preaching of Dr. Sacheverell; then the youth, victorious in school, carried aloft in triumph by his admiring comrades; and, finally, the renowned scholar and author, in the meridian of his greatness, standing bareheaded in the market-place of Uttoxeter, doing penance for his undutiful refusal, when a lad, to relieve his weary, infirm father in the work of tending the bookstall at that place. Every one knows that touching story, and no one who thinks of it when standing here will gaze with any feeling but that of reverence, commingled with the wish to lead a true and simple life, upon the noble, thoughtful face and figure of the great moralist, who now seems to look down with benediction upon the scenes of his innocent and happy youth. The statue, which is in striking contrast with the humble birthplace, points the expressive moral of a splendid career. No tablet has yet been placed on the house in which Johnson was born. Perhaps it is not needed. Yet surely this place, if any place on earth, ought to be preserved and protected as a literary shrine. Johnson was not a great creative poet; neither a Shakespeare, a Dryden, a Byron, or a Tennyson; but he was one of the most massive and majestic characters in English literature. A superb example of self-conquest and moral supremacy, a mine of extensive and diversified learning, an intellect remarkable for deep penetration and broad and sure grasp of the greatest subjects, he exerted, as few men have ever exerted, the original, elemental force of genius; and his immortal legacy to his fellow-men was an abiding influence for good. The world is better and happier because of him, and because of the many earnest characters and honest lives that his example has inspired; and this cradle of greatness ought to be saved and marked for every succeeding generation as long as time endures.

One of the interesting features of Lichfield is an inscription that vividly recalls the ancient strife of Roundhead and Cavalier, two centuries and a half ago. This is found upon a stone scutcheon, set in the wall over the door of the house that is No. 24 Dam street, and these are its words:—" March 2d, 1643, Lord Brooke, a General of the Parliament Forces preparing to Besiege the Close of Lichfield, then garrisoned For King Charles the First, Received his death-wound on the spot Beneath this Inscription, By a shot in the forehead from Mr. Dyott, a gentleman who had placed himself on the Battlements of the great steeple, to annoy the Besiegers." One of them he must have "annoyed" seriously. It was "a long shot, Sir Lucius," for, standing on the place of that catastrophe and looking up to "the battlements of the great steeple," it seemed to have covered a distance of nearly four hundred feet. Other relics of those Roundhead wars were shown in the cathedral, in an ancient room now used for the bishop's consistory court — these being two cannon-balls (fourteen-pounders) and the ragged and rusty fragments of a shell that were dug out of the ground near the church a few years ago. Many of these practical tokens of Puritan zeal have been discovered. Lichfield cathedral close, in the time of Bishop Walter de Langton, who died in 1321, was surrounded with a wall and fosse, and thereafter whenever the wars came it was used as a fortification. In the Stuart times it was often besieged. Sir John Gell succeeded Lord Brooke, when the latter had been shot by Mr. Dyott — who is said to have been "deaf and dumb," but who certainly was not blind. The close was surrendered on March 5, 1643, and thereupon the Parliamentary victors, according to their ruthless and brutal custom, straightway ravaged the church, tearing the brasses from the tombs, breaking the effigies, and utterly despoiling beauty which it had taken generations of pious zeal and loving devotion to create. The great spire was battered down by those vandals, and in falling it wrecked the chapter-house. The noble church, indeed, was made a ruin — and so it remained till 1661, when its munificent benefactor, Bishop Hackett, began its restoration, now happily almost complete. Prince Rupert captured Lichfield close for the king in April 1643, and General Lothian recovered it for the Parliament in the summer of 1646, after which time it was completely dismantled. Charles I. came to this place after the fatal battle of Naseby, and sad enough that picturesque, vacillating, shortsighted, beatific aristocrat must have been, gazing over the green fields of Lichfield, to know — as surely even he must then have known — that his cause was doomed, if not entirely lost.

It will not take you long to traverse Lichfield, and you may ramble all around it through little green lanes between hedgerows. This you will do if you are wise, for the walk, especially at evening, is peaceful and lovely. The wanderer never gets far away from the cathedral. Those three superb spires steadily dominate the scene, and each new view of them seems fairer than the last. All around this little city the fields are richly green, and many trees diversify the prospect. Pausing to rest awhile in the mouldering graveyard of old St. Chad's, I saw the rooks flocking homeward to the great tree-tops not far away, and heard their many querulous, sagacious, humorous croakings, while over the distance, borne upon the mild and fragrant evening breeze, floated the solemn note of a warning bell from the minster tower, as the shadows deepened and the night came down. Scenes like this sink deep into the heart, and memory keeps them forever.

XVI.

FROM LONDON TO EDINBURGH.

EDINBURGH, September 9, 1889. — Scotland again, and never more beautiful than now! The harvest moon is shining upon the grim old castle, and the bagpipes are playing under my windows to-night. It has been a lovely day. The train rolled out of King's Cross, London, at ten this morning, and it rolled into Waverley, Edinburgh, about seven to-night. The trip by the Great Northern railway is one of the most interesting journeys that can be made in England. At first indeed the scenery is not striking; but even at first you are whirled past spots of exceptional historic and literary interest — among them the battlefield of Barnet, and the old church and graveyard of Hornsey where Tom Moore buried his little daughter Barbara, and where the venerable poet Samuel Rogers sleeps the last sleep. Soon these are gone, and presently, dashing through a flat country, you get a clear view of Peterborough cathedral, massive, dark, and splendid, with its graceful cone-shaped pinnacles, its vast square central tower, and the three great pointed and recessed arches that adorn its west front. This church contains the dust of Queen Katherine, the Spanish wife of Henry VIII., who died at Kimbolton Castle, Huntingdonshire, in 1535; and there the remains of Mary Stuart were first buried (1587), — resting there a long time before her son, James I., conveyed them to Westminster Abbey. Both those queens were buried by one and the same gravedigger — that famous sexton, old Scarlett, whose portrait is in the cathedral, and who died July 2, 1591, aged ninety-eight.

The country is so level that the receding tower of Peterborough remains for a long time in sight, but soon, — as the train speeds through pastures of clover and through fields of green and red and yellow herbage, divided by glimmering hedges and diversified with red-roofed villages and gray churchtowers, — the land grows hilly, and long white roads are visible stretching away like bands of silver over the lonely hill-tops. Figures of gleaners are seen, now and then, scattered through fields whence the harvest has lately been gathered. Sheep are feeding in the pastures, and cattle are couched under fringes of wood. The bright emerald of the sod sparkles with the golden yellow of the colt's-foot, and sometimes the scarlet waves of the poppy come tumbling into the plain like a cataract of fire. Windmills spread their whirling sails upon the summits round about, and over the nestling ivy-clad cottages and over the stately trees there are great flights of rooks. A gray sky broods above, faintly suffused with sunshine, but there is no glare and no heat, and often the wind is laden with a fragrance of wildflowers and of hay.

It is noon at Grantham, where there is just time enough to see that this is a flourishing city of red-brick houses and fine spacious streets, with a lofty, spired church, and far away eastward a high line of hills. Historic Newark is presently reached and passed — a busy, contented town, smiling through the sunshine and mist, and as it fades in the distance I remember that we are leaving Lincoln, with its glorious cathedral, to the southeast, and to the west Newstead Abbey, Annesley, Southwell, and Hucknall-Torkard — places memorably associated with the poet Byron and dear to the heart of every lover of poetic literature. At Markham the country is exceedingly pretty, with woods and hills over which multitudes of rooks and starlings are in full career, dark, rapid, and garrulous. About Bawtry the land is flat, and flat it continues to be until we have sped a considerable way beyond York. But in the meantime we flash through opulent Doncaster, famed for manufactories and for horse-races, rosy and active amid the bright green fields. There are not many trees in this region, and as we draw near Selby — a large red-brick city upon the banks of a broad river — its massive old church-tower looms conspicuous under smoky skies. In the outskirts of this town there are cosy houses clad with ivy, in which the pilgrim might well be pleased to linger. But there is no pause, and in a little while magnificent York bursts upon the view, stately and glorious, under a black sky that is full of driving clouds. The minster stands out like a mountain, and the giant towers rear themselves in solemn majesty — the grandest piece of church architecture in England! The brimming Ouse shines as if it were a stream of liquid ebony. The meadows around the city glow like living emeralds, while the harvest-fields are stored and teeming with stacks of golden grain. Great flights of startled doves people the air — as white as snow under the sable fleeces of the driving storm. I had seen York under different guises, but never before under a sky at once so sombre and so romantic.

We bear toward Thirsk now, leaving behind us, westward of our track, old Ripon, in the distance, memorable for many associations, and cherished in theatrical annals as the place of the death and burial of the distinguished founder of the Jefferson family of actors. Bleak Haworth is not far distant, and remembrance of it prompts many reverent thoughts of the strange genius of Charlotte Brontë. Darlington is the next important place, a town of manufacture, conspicuous for its tall, smoking chimneys and evidently prosperous. This is the land of stone walls and stone cottages — the grim precinct of Durham. The country is cultivated, but rougher than the Midlands, and the essentially diversified character of this small island is once again impressed upon your mind. All through this region there are little white-walled houses with red roofs. At Ferry Hill the scenery changes again and becomes American — a mass of rocky gorges and densely wooded ravines. All trace of storm has vanished by this time, and when, after a brief interval of eager expectation, the noble towers of Durham cathedral sweep into the prospect, that suburb monument of ancient devotion, together with all the dark gray shapes of that pictorial city — so magnificently placed, in an abrupt precipitous gorge, on both sides of the brimming Weir — are seen under a sky of the softest Italian blue, dappled with white clouds of drifting fleece. Durham is all too quickly passed — fading away in a landscape sweetly mellowed by a faint blue mist. Then stately rural mansions are seen, half hidden among great trees. Wreaths of smoke curl upward from scattered dwellings all around the circle of the hills. Each distant summit is seen to be crowned with a tower or a town. A fine castle springs into view just before Birtley glances by, and we see that this is a place of woodlands, piquant with a little of the roughness of unsophisticated nature. But the scene changes suddenly, as in a theatre, and almost in a moment the broad and teeming Tyne blazes beneath the scorching summer sun, and the gray houses of Gateshead and

Newcastle fill the picture with life and motion. The waves glance and sparkle — a wide plain of shimmering silver. The stream is alive with shipping. There is movement everywhere, and smoke and industry and traffic — and doubtless noise, though we are on a height and cannot hear it. A busier scene could not be found in all this land, nor one more strikingly representative of the industrial character and interests of England.

After leaving Newcastle we glide past a gentle, winding ravine, thickly wooded on both its sides, with a bright stream glancing in its depth. The meadows all around are green, fresh, and smiling, and soon our road skirts by beautiful Morpeth, bestriding a dark and lovely river and crouched in a bosky dell. At Widdrington the land shelves downward, the trees become sparse, and you catch a faint glimpse of the sea — the broad blue wilderness of the Northern Ocean. From this point onward the panorama is one of perfect and unbroken loveliness. Around you are spacious meadows of fern, diversified with clumps of fir-trees, and the sweet wind that blows upon your face seems glad and buoyant with its exultant vitality. At Warkworth Castle the ocean view is especially magnificent — the brown and red sails of the ships and various craft descried at sea contributing to the prospect a lovely element of picturesque character. Alnwick, with its storied associations of "the Percy out of Northumberland," is left to the westward, while on the east the romantic village of Alnmouth woos the traveller with an irresistible charm. No one who has once seen that exquisite place can ever be content without seeing it again — and yet there is no greater wisdom in the conduct of life than to avoid forever a second sight of any spot where you have once been happy. This village, with its little lighthouse and graceful steeple, is built upon a promontory in the sea, and is approached over the sands by a long, isolated road across the bridge of four fine arches. All the country-side in this region is rich. At Long Houghton a grand church uprears its vast square tower, lonely and solemn in its place of graves. Royal Berwick comes next, stately and serene upon its ocean crag, with the white-crested waves curling on its beach and the glad waters of the Tweed kissing the fringes of its sovereign mantle as they rush into the sea. The sun is sinking now, and over the many-coloured meadows, red and brown and golden and green, the long, thin shadows of the trees slope eastward and softly hint the death of day. The sweet breeze of evening stirs the long grasses, and on many a gray stone house shakes the late pink and yellow roses and makes the ivy tremble. It is Scotland now, and as we pass through the storied Border we keep the ocean almost constantly in view — losing it for a little while at Dunbar, but finding it again at Drem — till, past the battlefield of Prestonpans and past the quaint villages of Cockenzie and Musselburgh and the villas of Portobello, we come slowly to a pause in the shadow of Arthur's Seat, where the great lion crouches over the glorious city of Edinburgh.

XVII.

INTO THE HIGHLANDS.

LOCH AWE, SEPTEMBER 14, 1889. — Under a soft gray sky, and through fields that still are slumbering in the early morning mist, the train rolls out of Edinburgh, bound to the north. The wind blows gently; the air is cool; strips of thin, fleecy cloud are driving over the distant hill-tops, and the birds are flying low. The track is by Queensferry, and in that region many little low stone cottages are seen, surrounded with simple gardens of flowers. For a long time the train runs through a deep ravine, with rocky banks on either hand, but presently it emerges into pastures where the sheep are grazing, and into fields in which the late harvest stands garnered in many graceful sheaves. Tall chimneys, vigorously smoking, are visible here and there in the distant landscape. The fat, black rooks are taking their morning flight, clamouring as they go. Stone houses with red roofs glide into the picture, and a graceful church-spire rises on a remote hill-top. In all directions there are trees, but they seem of recent growth, for no one of them is large. Soon the old cattle-market town of Falkirk springs up in the prospect, girt with fine hills and crested with masses of white and black smoke that is poured upward from the many tall chimneys of its busy ironworks. The houses here are made of gray stone and of red brick, and many of them are large, square buildings, seemingly commodious and opulent. A huge cemetery, hemmed in with trees and shrubs, is seen to skirt the city. Carron River, with its tiny but sounding cataract, is presently passed, and at Larbert your glance rests lovingly upon "the little gray church on the windy hill." North of this place, beyond the Forth, the country in the distance is mountainous, while all the intermediate region is rich with harvest-fields. Kinnaird lies to the eastward, while northward a little way is the famous field of Bannockburn. Two miles more and the train pauses in "gray Stirling," glorious with associations of historic splendour and ancient romance. The Castle of Stirling is not as ruggedly grand as that of Edinburgh, but it is a noble architectural pile, and it is nobly placed on a great crag fronting the vast mountains and the gloomy heavens of the north. The best view of it is obtained looking at it southward, and as I gazed upon it, under the cold and frowning sky, the air was populous with many birds that circled around its cone-shaped turrets, and hovered over the plain below, while across the distant mountain-tops, east, west, and north, dark and ragged masses of mist were driven in wild, tempestuous flight. Speeding onward now, along the southern bank of the Forth, the traveller takes a westerly course, past Gargunnock and Kippen, seeing little villages of gray stone cottages nestled in the hill-gaps, distant mountain-sides, clad with furze, dark patches of woodland, and moors of purple heather commingled with meadows of brilliant green. The sun breaks out, for a few moments, and the sombre hue of the gray sky is lightened with streaks of gold. At Bucklyvie there is a second pause, and then the course is northwest, through banks and braes of heather, to peaceful Aberfoyle and the mountains of Menteith.

The characteristic glory of the Scottish hills is the infinite variety and beauty of their shapes and the loveliness of their colour. The English mountains and lakes in Westmoreland and Cumberland possess a sweeter and softer grace, and are more calmly and wooingly beautiful; but the Scottish mountains and lakes excel them in grandeur, majesty, and romance. It would be presumption to undertake to describe the solemn austerity, the lofty and lonely magnificence, the bleak, weird, haunted isolation, and the fairy-like fantasy of this poetic realm; but a lover of it may declare his passion and speak his sense of its enthralling and bewitching charm. Sir Walter Scott's spirited and trenchant lines on the emotion of the patriot sang themselves over and over in my thought, and were wholly and grandly ratified, as the coach rolled up the mountain road, ever climbing height after height, while new and ever new prospects continually unrolled themselves before delighted eyes, on the familiar but always novel journey from Aberfoyle to the Trosachs. That mountain road, on its upward course, and during most part of the way, winds through treeless pastureland, and in every direction, as your vision ranges, you behold other mountains equally bleak, save for the bracken and the heather, among which the sheep wander and the grouse nestle in concealment, or whir away on frightened wings. Ben Lomond, wrapt in straggling mists, was dimly visible far to the west; Ben A'an towered conspicuous in the foreground; and further north Ben Ledi heaved its broad mass and rugged sides to heaven. Loch Vennacher, seen for a few moments, shone like a diamond set in emeralds, and as we gazed we seemed to see the bannered barges of Roderick Dhu and to hear the martial echoes of "Hail to the Chief." Loch Achray glimmered forth for an instant under the gray sky, as when "the small birds would not sing aloud" and the wrath equally of tempest and of war hung silently above it in one awful moment of suspense. There was a sudden and dazzling vision of Loch Katrine, and then all prospect was broken, and, rolling down among the thickly wooded dwarf hills that give the name of Trosachs to this place, we were lost in the masses of fragrant foliage that girdle and adorn in perennial verdure the hallowed scene of *The Lady of the Lake.*

Loch Katrine is another Lake Horicon, with a grander environment, and this — like all the Scottish lakes — has the advantage of a more evenly sharp and vigorous air and of leaden and frowning skies (in which, nevertheless, there is a peculiar, penetrating light), that darken their waters and impart to them a dangerous aspect that yet is strangely beautiful. As we swept past "Ellen's Island" and Fitz-James's "Silver Strand" I was grateful to see them in the mystery of this gray light and not in the garish sunshine. All around this sweet lake are the sentinel mountains,— Ben Venue rising in the south, Ben A'an in the east, and all the castellated ramparts that girdle Glen Finglas in the north. The eye dwells enraptured upon the circle of the hills; but by this time the imagination is so acutely stimulated, and the mind is so filled with glorious sights and exciting and ennobling reflections, that the sense of awe is tempered with a pensive sadness, and you feel yourself rebuked and humbled by the final and effectual lesson of man's insignificance that is taught by the implacable vitality of these eternal mountains. It is a relief to be brought back for a little to common life, and this relief you find in the landing at Stronachlachar and the ensuing drive— across the narrow strip of the shire of Stirling that intervenes between Loch Katrine and Loch Lomond — to the port of Inversnaid. This drive is through a wild and picturesque country, but after the mountain road from Aberfoyle to the Trosachs it could not well seem otherwise than calm — at least till the final descent into the vale of Inversnaid. From Inversnaid there is a short sail upon the northern waters of Loch Lomond — forever haunted by the shaggy presence of Rob Roy and the fierce and terrible image of Helen Macgregor — and then, landing at Ardlui, you drive past Inverarnan and hold a northern course to Crianlarich, traversing the vale of the Falloch and skirting along the western slope of the grim and gloomy Grampians — on which for miles and miles no human habitation is seen, nor any living creature save the vacant, abject sheep. The mountains are everywhere now, brown with bracken and purple with heather, stony, rugged, endless, desolate, and still with a stillness that is awful in its pitiless sense of inhumanity and utter isolation. At Crianlarich the railway is found again, and thence you whirl onward through lands of Breadalbane and Argyle to the proud mountains of Glen Orchy and the foot of that loveliest of all the lovely waters of Scotland — the ebony crystal of Loch Awe. The night is deepening over it as I write these words. The dark and solemn mountains that guard it stretch away into the mysterious distance and are lost in the shuddering gloom. The gray clouds have drifted by, and the cold, clear stars of autumnal heaven are reflected in its crystal depth, unmarred by even the faintest ripple upon its surface. A few small boats, moored to anchored buoys, float motionless upon it a little way from shore. There, on its lonely island, dimly visible in the fading light, stands the gray ruin of Kilchurn. A faint whisper comes from the black woods that fringe the mountain base, and floating from far across this lonely, haunted water there is a drowsy bird-note that calls to silence and to sleep.

XVIII.

HIGHLAND BEAUTIES.

OBAN, SEPTEMBER 17, 1889. — Seen in the twilight, as I first saw it, Oban is a pretty and picturesque seaside village, gay with glancing lights and busy with the movements of rapid vehicles and expeditious travellers. It is called the capital of the Western Highlands, and no doubt it deserves the name, for it is the common centre of all the trade and enterprise of this region, and all the threads of travel radiate from it. Built in a semicircle, along the margin of a lovely sheltered bay, it looks forth upon the wild waters of the Firth of Lorn, visible, southwesterly, through the sable sound of Kerrera, while behind and around it rises a bold range of rocky and sparsely wooded hills. On these are placed a few villas, and on a point toward the north stand the venerable, ivy-clad ruins of Dunolly Castle, in the ancestral domain of the ancient Highland family of Macdougall.

The houses of Oban are built of gray stone and are mostly modern. There are many hotels fronting upon the Parade, which extends for a long distance upon the verge of the sea. The opposite shore is Kerrera, an island about a mile distant, and beyond that island, and beyond Lorn water, extends the beautiful island of Mull, confronting iron-ribbed Morven. In many ways Oban is suggestive of an American seaport upon the New England coast. Various characteristics mark it that may be seen at Gloucester, Massachusetts (although that once romantic place has been spoiled by the Irish peasantry), and at Mount Desert in Maine. The surroundings, indeed, are different; for the Scottish hills have a delicious colour and a wildness all their own; while the skies, unlike those of blue and brilliant America, lower and gloom and threaten, and tinge the whole world beneath them — the moors, the mountains, the clustered gray villages, the lonely ruins, and the tumbling plains of the desolate sea — with a melancholy, romantic, shadowy darkness, the perfect twilight of poetic vision. No place could be more practical than Oban is, in its everyday life, nor any place more sweet and dreamlike to the pensive mood of contemplation and the roving gaze of fancy. Viewed, as I viewed it, under the starlight and the drifting cloud, between two and three o'clock this morning, it was a picture of beauty, never to be forgotten. A few lights were twinkling here and there among the dwellings, or momentarily flaring on the deserted Parade. No sound was heard but the moaning of the night-wind and the plash of waters softly surging on the beach. Now and then a belated passenger came wandering along the pavement and disappeared in a turn of the road. The air was sweet with the mingled fragrance of the heathery hills and the salt odours of the sea. Upon the glassy bosom of the bay — dark, clear, and gently undulating with the pressure of the ocean tide — more than seventy small boats, each moored at a buoy and all veered in one direction, swung careless on the water; and mingled with them were upward of twenty schooners and little steamboats, all idle and all at peace. Many an hour of toil and sorrow is yet to come before the long, strange journey of this life is ended; but the memory of that wonderful midnight moment, alone with the majesty of Nature, will be a solace in the darkest of them.

The Highland journey, from first to last, is an experience altogether novel and precious, and it is remembered with gratitude and delight. Before coming to Oban I gave two nights and days to Loch Awe — a place so beautiful and so fraught with the means of happiness that time stands still in it, and even "the ceaseless vulture" of care and regret ceases for a while to vex the spirit with remembrance of anything that is sad. Looking down from the summit of one of the great mountains that are the rich and rugged setting of this jewel, I saw the crumbling ruin of Kilchurn upon its little island, gray relic first of the Macgregors and then of the Campbells, who dispossessed them and occupied their realm. It must have been an imperial residence once. Its situation — cut off from the mainland and commanding a clear view, up the lake and down the valleys, southward and northward — is superb. No enemy could approach it unawares, and doubtless the followers of the Macgregor occupied every adjacent pass and were ambushed in every thicket on the heights. Seen from the neighbouring mountain-side the waters of Loch Awe are of such crystal clearness that near some part of the shore the white sands are visible in perfect outline beneath them, while all the glorious engirdling hills are reflected in their still and shining depth. Sometimes the sun flashed out and changed the waters to liquid silver, lighting up the gray ruin and flooding the mountain slopes with gold; but more often the skies kept their sombre hue, darkening all beneath them with a lovely gloom. All around were the beautiful hills of Glen Orchy, and far to the eastward great waves of white and leaden mist, slowly drifting in the upper ether, now hid and now disclosed the Olympian head of Ben Lui and the tangled hills of Glen Shirra and Glen Fyne. Close by, in its sweet vale of Sabbath stillness, was couched the little town of Dalmally, sole reminder of the presence of man in these remote solitudes, where Nature keeps the temple of her worship, and where words are needless to utter her glory and her praise. All day long the peaceful lake slumbered in placid beauty under the solemn sky — a few tiny boats and two little steamers swinging at anchor on its bosom. All day long the shadows of the clouds, commingled with flecks of sunshine, went drifting over the mountain. At nightfall two great flocks of sheep, each attended by the pensive shepherd in his plaid, and each guided and managed by those wonderfully intelligent collies that are a never-failing delight in these mountain lands, came slowly along the vale and presently vanished in Glen Strae. Nothing then broke the stillness but the sharp cry of the shepherd's dog and the sound of many cataracts, some hidden and some seen, that lapse in music and fall in many a mass of shattered silver and flying spray, through deep, rocky rifts down the mountain-side. After sunset a cold wind came on to blow, and soon the heavens were clear and "all the number of the stars" were mirrored in beautiful Loch Awe.

They speak of the southwestern extremity of this lake as the head of it. Loch Awe station, accordingly, is at its foot, near Kilchurn. Nevertheless, "where Macgregor sits is the head of the table," for the foot of the loch is lovelier than its head. And yet its head also is lovely, although in a less positive way. From Loch Awe station to Ford, a distance of twenty-six miles, you sail in a toy steamboat, sitting either on the open deck or in a cabin of glass and gazing at the panorama of the hills on either hand, some wooded and some bare, and all magnificent. A little after passing the mouth of the river Awe, which flows through the black Pass of Brander and unites with Loch Etive, I saw the double crest of great Ben Cruachan towering into the clouds and visible at intervals above them—the higher peak magnificently bold. It is a wild country all about this region, but here and there you see a little hamlet or a lone farm-house, and among the moorlands the occasional figure of a sportsman with his dog and gun. As the boat sped onward into the moorland district the mountains became great shapes of snowy crystal, under the sullen sky, and presently resolved into vast cloud-shadows, dimly outlined against the northern heavens, and seemingly based upon a sea of rolling vapour. The sail is past Inisdrynich, the island of the Druids, past Inishail and Inis Fraoch, and presently past the lovely ruin of Inischonnel Castle, called also Ardchonnel, facing southward, at the end of an island promontory, and covered thick with ivy. The landing is at Ford Pier, and about one mile from that point you may see a little inn, a few cottages crumbling in picturesque decay, and a diminutive kirk, that constitute the village of Ford My purpose here was to view an estate close by this village, now owned by Henry Bruce, Esq., but many years ago the domain of Alexander Campbell, an ancestor of my children, being their mother's grandsire; and not in all Scotland could be found a more romantic spot than the glen by the lochside that shelters the melancholy, decaying, haunted fabric of the old house of Ederline. Such a poet as Edgar Poe would have revelled in that place — and well he might! There is a new and grand mansion on higher ground in the park, but the ancient house, almost abandoned now, is a thousand times more characteristic and interesting than the new one. Both are approached through a long, winding avenue, overhung with great trees that interlace their branches above it and make a cathedral aisle; but soon the pathway to the older house turns aside into a grove of chestnuts, birches, and yews, — winding under vast dark boughs that bend like serpents completely to the earth and then ascend once more, — and so goes onward through sombre glades and through groves of rhododendron to the levels of Loch Ederline and the front of the mansion, now desolate and half in ruins. It was an old house a hundred years ago. It is covered with ivy and buried among the trees, and on its surface and on the tree-trunks around it the lichen and the yellow moss have gathered in rank luxuriance. The waters of the lake ripple upon a rocky landing almost at its door. Here once lived as proud a Campbell as ever breathed in Scotland, and here his haughty spirit wrought out for itself the doom of a lonely age and a broken heart. His grave is on a little island in the lake — a family burial-ground,[1] such as may often be found on ancient sequestered estates in the Highlands — where the tall trees wave above it and the weeds are growing thick upon its surface, while over it the rooks caw and clamour and the idle winds career, in heedless indifference that is sadder even than neglect. So destiny

---

[1] On the stone that marks this sepulchre are the following inscriptions, which may suitably be preserved in this chronicle: —

Alexander Campbell Esquire, of Ederline. Died 2d October, 1841. In his 76th year.

Matilda Campbell. Second daughter of William Campbell Esq., of Ederline. Died on the 21st Novr 1842. In her 6th year.

William Campbell, Esq. of Ederline. Died 15th January 1855, in his 42nd year.

Lachlan Aderson Campbell. His son. Died January 27th, 1859. In his 5th year.

[John Campbell, the eldest son of Alexander, died February 26, 1854, and is buried in the Necropolis, at Toronto, Canada.]

vindicates its inexorable edict and the great law of retribution is fulfilled. A stranger sits in his seat and rules in his hall, and of all the followers that once waited on his lightest word there remains but a single one — aged, infirm, and nearing the end of the long journey — to scrape the moss from his forgotten gravestone and to think sometimes of his ancient greatness and splendour, forever passed away. We rowed around Loch Ederline and looked down into its black waters (that in some parts have never been sounded, and are fabled to reach through to the other side of the world), and as our oars dipped and plashed the timid moorfowl scurried into the bushes and the white swans sailed away in haughty wrath, while, warned by gathering storm-clouds, multitudes of old rooks that long have haunted the place came flying overhead, with many a querulous croak, toward their nests in Ederline grove.

Back to Loch Awe station, and presently onward past the Falls of Cruachan and through the grim Pass of Brander — down which the waters of the Awe rush in a sable flood between jagged and precipitous cliffs for miles and miles — and soon we see the bright waves of Loch Etive smiling under a sunset sky, and the many bleak, brown hills that fringe Glen Lonan and range along to Oban and the verge of the sea. There will be an hour for rest and thought. It seems wild and idle to write about these things. Life in Scotland is deeper, richer, stronger and sweeter than any words could possibly be that any man could possibly expend upon it. The place is the natural home of imagination, romance, and poetry. Thought is grander here, and passion is wilder and more exuberant than on the velvet plains and among the chaste and stately elms of the South. The blood flows in a stormier torrent and the mind takes on something of the gloomy and savage majesty of those gaunt, barren, lonely hills. Even Sir Walter Scott, speaking of his own great works (which are precious beyond words, and must always be loved and cherished by readers who know what beauty is), said that all he had ever done was to polish the brasses that already were made. This is the soul of excellence in British literature, and this, likewise, is the basis of stability in British civilisation — that the country is lovelier than the loveliest poetry that ever was written about it or ever could be written about it, and that the land and the life possess an inherent fascination for the inhabitants that nothing else could supply, and that no influence can ever destroy or ever seriously disturb. Democracy is rife all over the world, but it will as soon impede the eternal courses of the stars as it will change the constitution or shake the social fabric of this realm. "Once more upon the waters — yet once more!" Soon upon the stormy billows of Lorn I shall see these lovely shores fade in the distance. Soon, merged again in the strife and tumult of the commonplace world, I shall murmur, with as deep a sorrow as the sad strain itself expresses, the tender words of Scott: —

> " Glenorchy's proud mountains,
> Kilchurn and her towers,
> Glenstrae and Glenlyon
> No longer are ours."

XIX.

THE HEART OF SCOTLAND.

" The Heart of Scotland, Britain's other eye." — BEN JONSON.

EDINBURGH, AUGUST 24, 1890. — A bright blue sky, across which many masses of thin white cloud are borne swiftly on the cool western wind, bends over the stately city, and all her miles of gray mansions and spacious, cleanly streets sparkle beneath it in a flood of summer sunshine. It is the Lord's Day, and most of the highways are deserted and quiet. From the top of the Calton Hill you look down upon hundreds of blue smoke-wreaths curling upward from the chimneys of the resting and restful town, and in every direction the prospect is one of opulence and peace. A thousand years of history are here crystallised within the circuit of a single glance, and while you gaze upon one of the grandest emblems that the world contains of a storied and romantic past, you behold likewise a living and resplendent pageant of the beauty of to-day. Nowhere else are the Past and the Present so lovingly blended. There, in the centre, towers the great crown of St. Giles. Hard by are the quaint slopes of the Canongate, — teeming with illustrious, or picturesque, or terrible figures of Long Ago. Yonder the glorious Castle Crag looks steadfastly westward, — its manifold, wonderful colours continuously changing in the changeful daylight. Down in the valley Holyrood, haunted by a myriad of memories and by one resplendent face and entrancing presence, nestles at the foot of the giant Salisbury Crag; while the dark, rivened peak of Arthur's Seat rears itself supremely over the whole stupendous scene. Southward and westward, in the distance, extends the bleak range of the Pentland Hills; eastward the cone of Berwick Law and the desolate Bass Rock seem to cleave the sea; and northward, beyond the glistening crystal of the Forth, — with the white lines of embattled Inchkeith like a diamond on its bosom, — the lovely Lomonds, the virginal mountain breasts of Fife, are bared to the kiss of heaven. It is such a picture as words can but faintly suggest; but when you look upon it you readily comprehend the pride and the passion with which a Scotsman loves his native land.

Dr. Johnson named Edinburgh as "a city too well known to admit description." That judgment was proclaimed more than a hundred years ago — before yet Caledonia had bewitched the world's heart as the haunted land of Robert Burns and Walter Scott — and if it were true then it is all the more true now. But while the reverent pilgrim along the ancient highways of history may not wisely attempt description, which would be superfluous, he perhaps may usefully indulge in brief chronicle and impression — for these sometimes prove suggestive to minds that are kindred with his own. Hundreds of travellers visit Edinburgh ; but it is one thing to visit and another thing to see ; and every suggestion, surely, is of value that helps to clarify our vision. This capital is not learned by driving about in a cab ; for Edinburgh to be truly seen and comprehended must be seen and comprehended as an exponent of the colossal individuality of the Scottish character ; and therefore it must be observed with thought. Here is no echo and no imitation. Many another provincial city of Britain in a miniature copy of London; but the quality of Edinburgh is her own. Portions of her architecture do indeed denote a reverence for ancient Italian models, while certain other portions reveal the influence of the semi-classical taste that prevailed in the time of the Regent, afterwards George IV. The democratic tendency of this period — expressing itself here precisely as it does everywhere else, in button-making pettiness and vulgar commonplace — is likewise sufficiently obvious. Nevertheless in every important detail of Edinburgh, and of its life, the reticent, resolute, formidable, impetuous, passionate character of the Scottish race is conspicuous and predominant. Much has been said against the Scottish spirit — the tide of cavil purling on from Dr. Johnson to Sydney Smith. Dignity has been denied to it, and so has magnanimity, and so has humour; but there is no audience more quick than the Scottish audience to respond either to pathos or to mirth; there is no literature in the world so musically, tenderly, and weirdly poetical as the Scottish literature; there is no place on earth where the imaginative instinct of the national mind has resisted, as it has resisted

THE HEART OF SCOTLAND. 257

in Scotland, the encroachment of utility upon the domain of romance; there is no people whose history has excelled that of Scotland in the display of heroic, intellectual, and moral purpose, combined with passionate sensibility; and no city could surpass the physical fact of Edinburgh as a manifestation of broad ideas, unstinted opulence, and grim and rugged grandeur. Whichever way you turn, and whatever object you behold, that consciousness is always present to your thought — the consciousness of a race of beings intensely original, individual, passionate, authoritative, and magnificent.

The capital of Scotland is not only beautiful but eloquent. The present writer does not assume to describe it, or to instruct the reader concerning it, but only to declare that at every step the sensitive mind is impressed with the splendid intellect, the individual force, and the romantic charm of the Scottish character, as it is commemorated and displayed in this delightful place. What a wealth of significance it possesses may be indicated by even the most meagre record and the most superficial commentary upon the passing events of a traveller's ordinary day. The greatest name in the literature of Scotland is Walter Scott. He lived and laboured for twenty-four years in the modest three-story, gray stone house which is No. 39 Castle street. It has been my privilege to enter that house, and to stand in the room in which Scott began the novel of *Waverley*. Many years roll backward under the spell of such an experience, and the gray-haired man is a boy again, with all the delights of the Waverley Novels before him, health shining in his eyes, and joy beating in his heart, as he looks onward through vistas of golden light into a paradise of fadeless flowers and of happy dreams. The room that was Scott's study is a small one, on the first floor, at the back, and is lighted by one large window, opening eastward, through which you look upon the rear walls of sombre, gray buildings, and upon a small slope of green lawn, in which is the unmarked grave of one of Sir Walter's dogs. "The misery of keeping a dog," he once wrote, "is his dying so soon; but, to be sure, if he lived for fifty years and then died, what would become of me?" My attention was called to a peculiar fastening on the window of the study, — invented and placed there by Scott himself, — so arranged that the sash can be safely kept locked when raised a few inches from the sill. On the south side of the room is the fireplace, facing which he would sit as he wrote, and into which, of an evening, he has often gazed, hearing meanwhile the moan of the winter wind, and conjuring up, in the blazing brands, those figures of brave knights and gentle ladies that were to live forever in the amber of his magical art. Next to the study, on the same floor, is the larger apartment that was his dining-room, where his portrait of Claverhouse (now at Abbotsford) once hung above the mantel, and where so many of the famous people of the past enjoyed his hospitality and his talk. On the south wall of this room now hang two priceless autograph letters, one of them in the handwriting of Scott, the other in that of Burns. Both rooms are used for business offices now, — the house being tenanted by the agency of the New-Zealand Mortgage Company, — and both are furnished with large presses for the custody of deeds and family archives. Nevertheless these rooms remain much as they were when Scott lived in them, and his spirit seems to haunt the place. I was brought very near to him that day, for in the same hour was placed in my hands the original manuscript of his *Journal,* and I saw, in his own handwriting, the last words that ever fell from his pen. That *Journal* is in two quarto volumes. One of them is filled with writing; the other half filled; and the lines in both are of a fine, small character, crowded closely together. Toward the last the writing manifests only too well the growing infirmity of the broken Minstrel — the forecast of the hallowed deathbed of Abbotsford and the venerable and glorious tomb of Dryburgh. These are his last words: " We slept reasonably, but on the next morning " — and so the *Journal* abruptly ends. I can in no way express the emotion with which I looked upon those feebly scrawled syllables — the last effort of the nerveless hand that once had been strong enough to thrill the heart of all the world. The *Journal* has been lovingly and carefully edited by David Douglas, whose fine taste and great gentleness of nature, together with his ample knowledge of Scottish literature and society, eminently qualify him for the performance of this sacred duty; and the world will possess this treasure and feel the charm of its beauty and pathos — which is the charm of a great nature expressed in its perfect simplicity; but the spell that is cast upon the heart and the imagination by a prospect of the actual handwriting of Sir Walter Scott, in the last words that he wrote, cannot be conveyed in print.

From the house in Castle street I went to the rooms of the Royal Society, where there is a portrait of Scott, by John Graham Gilbert, more life-like — being representative of his soul as well as his face and person — than any other that is known. It hangs there, in company with other paintings of former presidents of this institution, — notably one of Sir David Brewster and one of James Watt, — in the hall in which Sir Walter often sat, presiding over the deliberations and literary exercises of his comrades in scholarship and art. In another hall I saw the pulpit in which John Knox used to preach, in the old days of what Dr. Johnson expressively called "The ruffians of Reformation," and hard by was "The Maiden," the terrible Scottish guillotine, with its great square knife set in a thick weight of lead, by which the grim Regent Morton was slain in 1581, the Marquis of Argyle in 1661, and the gallant, magnanimous, devoted Earl of Argyle in

1685 — one more sacrifice to the insatiate House of Stuart. This monster has drunk the blood of many a noble gentleman, and there is a weird, sinister suggestion of gratified ferocity and furtive malignity in its rude, grisly, uncanny fabric of blackened timbers. You may see in the quaint little panelled chapel of St. Mary Magdalen, not many steps distant from the present abode of the sanguinary "Maiden," — brooding over her hideous consummation of slaughter and misery, — the place where the mangled body of the heroic Earl of Argyle was laid, in secret sanctuary, for several nights after that scene of piteous sacrifice at the old Market Cross; and when you walk in the solemn enclosure of the Greyfriars church, — so fitly styled by Sir Walter "The Westminster Abbey of Scotland," — your glance will fall upon a sunken pillar, low down upon the northern slope of that haunted, lamentable ground, which bears the letters " I. M.," and which marks the grave of the baleful Morton, whom the Maiden decapitated for his share in the murder of Rizzio. In these old cities there is no keeping away from sepulchres. "The paths of glory," in every sense, "lead but to the grave." George Buchanan and Allan Ramsay (poets whom no literary pilgrim will neglect) rest in this churchyard, though the exact places of their interment are not positively denoted, and here, likewise, rest the elegant historian Robertson, and "the Addison of Scotland," Henry Mackenzie. The building in the High street in which Allan Ramsay once had his abode and his bookshop, and in which he wrote his pastoral of *The Gentle Shepherd*, is occupied now by a barber; but since he is one that scorns not to proclaim over his door in mighty letters the poetic lineage of his dwelling it seems not amiss that this haunt of the Muses should have fallen into such pious though lowly hands. Of such a character, hallowed with associations that pique the fancy and touch the heart, are the places and the names that an itinerant continually encounters in his rambles in Edinburgh.

One could muse for many an hour over the little Venetian mirror that hangs in the bedroom of Mary Stuart in Holyrood Palace. What faces and what scenes it must have reflected! How often her own beautiful countenance and person — the dazzling eyes, the snowy brow, the red gold hair, the alabaster bosom — may have blazed in its crystal depths, now tarnished and dim, like the record of her own calamitous and wretched days! Did those lovely eyes look into this mirror — and was their glance scared and tremulous, or fixed and terrible — on that dismal February night, so many years ago, when the fatal explosion in the Kirk o' Field resounded with an echo that has never died away? Who can tell? This glass saw the gaunt and livid face of Ruthven when he led his comrades of murder into that royal chamber, and it beheld Rizzio screaming in mortal terror as he was torn from the skirts of his mistress and savagely slain before her eyes. Perhaps, also, when that hideous episode was over and done with, it saw Queen Mary and her despicable husband the next time they met and were alone together in that ghastly room. "It shall be dear blood to some of you," the queen had said, while the murder of Rizzio was doing. Surely, having so injured a woman, any man with eyes to see might have divined his fate, in the perfect calm of her heavenly face and the quiet tones of her gentle voice, at such a moment as that. "At the fireside tragedies are acted" — and tragic enough must have been the scene of that meeting, apart from human gaze, in the chamber of crime and death.

No other relic of Mary Stuart stirs the imagination as that mirror does — unless, perhaps, it be the little ebony crucifix, once owned and reverenced by Sir Walter Scott and now piously treasured at Abbotsford, which she held in her hands when she went to her death in the hall of Fotheringay Castle.

Holyrood Palace, in Mary Stuart's time, was not of its present shape. The tower containing her rooms was standing, and from that tower the building extended eastward to the abbey, and then it veered to the south. Much of this building was destroyed by fire in 1544, and again in Cromwell's time, but both church and palace were rebuilt. The entire south side, with its tower that looks directly towards the crag, was added in the later period of Charles II. The furniture in Mary Stuart's room is mostly spurious, but the rooms are genuine. Musing thus, and much striving to reconstruct those strange scenes of the past, in which that beautiful, dangerous woman bore so great a part, the pilgrim strolls away into the Cannongate, — once clean and elegant, now squalid and noisome, — and still the storied figures of history walk by his side or come to meet him at every close and wynd. John Knox, Robert Burns, Tobias Smollett, David Hume, Dugald Stuart, John Wilson, Hugh Miller — Gay, led onward by the blithe and gracious Duchess of Queensberry, and Dr. Johnson, escorted by the affectionate and faithful James Boswell, the best biographer that ever lived,— these and many more, the lettered worthies of long ago, throng into this haunted street and glorify it with the rekindled splendours of other days. You cannot be lonely here. This it is that makes the place so eloquent and so precious. For what did those men live and labour? To what were their shining talents and wonderful forces devoted? To the dissemination of learning; to the emancipation of the human mind from the bondage of error; to the ministry of the beautiful — and thus to the advancement of the human race in material comfort, in gentleness of thought, in charity of conduct, in refinement of manners, and in that spiritual exaltation by which, and only by which, the true progress of mankind is at once accomplished and proclaimed.

But the dark has come, and this Edinburgh ramble shall end with the picture that closed its own magnificent day. You are standing on the rocky summit of Arthur's Seat. From that superb mountain peak your gaze takes in the whole capital, together with the country in every direction for many miles around. The evening is uncommonly clear. Only in the west dense masses of black cloud are thickly piled upon each other, through which the sun is sinking, red and sullen with menace of the storm. Elsewhere and overhead the sky is crystal, and of a pale, delicate blue. A cold wind blows briskly from the east and sweeps a million streamers of white smoke in turbulent panic over the darkening roofs of the city, far below. In the north the lovely Lomond Hills are distinctly visible across the dusky level of the Forth, which stretches away toward the ocean, one broad sheet of glimmering steel — its margin indented with many a graceful bay, and the little islands that adorn it shining like stones of amethyst set in polished flint. A few brown sails are visible, dotting the waters, and far to the east appears the graceful outline of the Isle of May, — which was the shrine of the martyred St. Adrian, — and the lonely, wave-beaten Bass Rock, with its millions of seagulls and solan geese. Busy Leith and picturesque Newhaven and every little village on the coast is sharply defined in the frosty light. At your feet is St. Leonards, with the tiny cottage of Jeanie Deans. Yonder, in the south, are the gray ruins of Craigmillar Castle—once the favourite summer home of the Queen of Scots, now open to sun and rain, mossgrown and desolate, and swept by every wind that blows. More eastward the eye lingers upon Carberry Hill, where Mary surrendered herself to her nobles just before the romantic episode of Loch Leven Castle; and far beyond that height the sombre fields, intersected by green hawthorn hedges and many-coloured with the various hues of pasture and harvest, stretch away to the hills of Lammermoor and the valleys of Tweed and Esk. Darker and darker grow the gathering shadows of the gloaming. The lights begin to twinkle in the city streets. The echoes of the rifles die away in the Hunter's Bog. A piper far off is playing the plaintive music of *The Blue Bells of Scotland*. And as your steps descend the crag the rising moon, now nearly at the full, shines through a gauzy mist and hangs above the mountain like a shield of gold upon the towered citadel of night.

XX.

SIR WALTER SCOTT.

MORE than a century has passed since Walter Scott was born — a poet destined to exercise a profound, far-reaching, permanent influence upon the feelings of the human race, and thus to act a conspicuous part in its moral and spiritual development and guidance. To the greatness of his mind, the nobility of his spirit, and the beauty of his life there is abundant testimony in his voluminous and diversified writings, and in his ample and honest biography. Everybody who reads has read something from the pen of Scott, or something commemorative of him, and in every mind to which his name is known it is known as the synonym of great faculties and wonderful achievement. There must have been enormous vitality of spirit, prodigious power of intellect, irresistible charm of personality, and lovable purity of moral nature in the man whom thousands that never saw him living — men and women of a later age and different countries — know and remember and love as Sir Walter Scott. Others have written greatly. Milton, Dryden, Addison, Pope, Cowper, Johnson, Wordsworth, Coleridge, Landor, — these are only a few of the imperial names that cannot die. But these names live in the world's respect. The name of Scott lives in its affection. What other name of the past in English literature — unless it be that of Shakespeare — arouses such a deep and sweet feeling of affectionate interest, gentle pleasure, gratitude, and reverential love?

The causes of Sir Walter Scott's ascendency are to be found in the goodness of his heart; the integrity of his conduct; the romantic and picturesque accessories and atmosphere of his life; the fertile brilliancy of his literary execution; the charm that he exercises, both as man and artist, over the imagination; the serene, tranquillising spirit of his works; and, above all, the buoyancy, the happy freedom, of his genius. He was not simply an intellectual power; he was also a human and gentle comforter. He wielded an immense mental force, but he always wielded it for good, and always with tenderness. It is impossible to conceive of his ever having done a wrong act, or of any contact with his influence that would not inspire the wish to be virtuous and noble. The scope of his sympathy was as broad as the weakness and the need are of the human race. He understood the hardship, the dilemma, in the moral condition of mankind: he wished people to be patient and cheerful, and he tried to make them so. His writings are full of sweetness and cheer, and they contain nothing that is morbid, — nothing that tends toward surrender and misery. He did not sequester himself in mental pride, but simply and sturdily, through years of conscientious toil, he employed the faculties of a strong, tender, gracious genius for the good of his fellow-creatures. The world loves him because he is worthy to be loved, and because he has lightened the burden of its care and augmented the sum of its happiness.

Certain differences and confusions of opinion have arisen from the consideration of his well-known views as to the literary art, together with his equally well-known ambition to take and to maintain the rank and estate of a country squire. As an artist he had ideals that he was never able to fulfil. As a man, and one who was influenced by imagination, taste, patriotism, family pride, and a profound belief in established monarchical institutions, it was natural that he should wish to found a grand and beautiful home for himself and his posterity. A poet is not the less a poet because he thinks modestly of his writings and practically knows and admits that there is something else in the world beside literature; or because he happens to want his dinner and a roof to cover him. In trying to comprehend a great man, a good method is to look at his life as a whole, and not to deduce petty inferences from the distorted interpretation of petty details. Sir Walter Scott's conduct of life, like the character out of which it sprang, was simple and natural. In all that he did you may perceive the influence of imagination acting upon the finest reason; the involuntary consciousness of reserve power; habitual deference to the voice of duty; an aspiring and picturesque plan of artistic achievement and personal distinction; and deep knowledge of the world. If ever there was a man who lived to be and not to seem, that man was Sir Walter Scott. He made no pretensions. He claimed nothing, but he quietly and earnestly earned all. His means were the oldest and the best ; self-respect, hard work, and fidelity to duty. The development of his nature was slow, but it was thorough and it was salutary. He was not hampered by precocity and he was not spoiled by conceit. He acted according to himself, honouring his individuality and obeying the inward monitor of his genius. But, combined with the delicate instinct of a gentleman, he had the wise insight, foresight, and patience of a philosopher ; and therefore he respected the individuality of others, the established facts of life, and the settled conventions of society. His mind was neither embittered by revolt nor sickened by delusion. Having had the good fortune to be born in a country in which a right plan of government prevails — the idea of the family — the idea of the strong central power at the head, with all other powers subordinated to it, — he felt no impulse toward revolution, no desire to regulate all things anew ; and he did not suffer perturbation from the feverish sense of being surrounded with uncertainty and endangered by exposure to popular caprice. During the period of immaturity, and notwithstanding physical weakness and pain, his spirit was kept equable and cheerful, not less by the calm environment of a permanent civilisation than by the clearness of his perceptions and the sweetness of his temperament. In childhood and youth he endeared himself to all who came near him, winning affection by inherent goodness and charm. In riper years that sweetness was reinforced by great sagacity, which took broad views of individual and social life; so that both by knowledge and by impulse he was a serene and happy man.

The quality that first impresses the student of the character and the writings of Sir Walter Scott is truthfulness. He was genuine. Although a poet, he suffered no torment from vague aspirations. Although once, and miserably, a disappointed lover, he permitted no morbid repining. Although the most successful author of his time, he displayed no egotism. To the end of his days he was frank and simple — not indeed sacrificing the reticence of a dignified, self-reliant nature, but suffering no blight from success, and wearing illustrious honours with spontaneous, unconscious grace. This truthfulness — the consequence and the sign of integrity and of great breadth of intellectual vision — moulded Sir Walter Scott's ambition and stamped the practical results of his career. A striking illustration of this is seen in his first adventure in literature. The poems originally sprang from the spontaneous action of the poetic impulse and faculty; but they were put forth modestly, in order that the author might guide himself according to the response of the public mind. He knew that he might fail as an author, but for failure of that sort, although he was intensely ambitious, he had no dread. There would always remain to him the career of private duty and the life of a gentleman. This view of him gives the key to his character and explains his conduct. Neither amid the experimental vicissitudes of his youth, nor amid the labours, achievements, and splendid honours of his manhood, did he ever place the imagination above the conscience, or brilliant writing above virtuous living, or art and fame above morality and religion. "I have been, perhaps, the most voluminous author of the day," he said, toward the close of his life; "and it is a comfort to me to think that I have tried to unsettle no man's faith, to corrupt no man's principles, and that I have written nothing which, on my deathbed, I should wish blotted." When at last he lay upon that deathbed the same thought animated and sustained him. "My dear," he said, to Lockhart, "be a good man, be virtuous, be religious — be a good man. Nothing else will give you any comfort when you come to lie here." The mind which thus habitually dwelt upon goodness as the proper object of human ambition and the chief merit of human life was not likely to vaunt itself on its labours or to indulge any save a modest and chastened pride in its achievements.

And this view of him explains the affectionate reverence with which the memory of Sir Walter Scott is cherished. He was pre-eminently a type of the greatness that is associated with virtue. But his virtue was not decorum and it was not goodyism. He does not, with Addison, represent elegant austerity; and he does not, with Montgomery, represent amiable tameness. His goodness was not insipid. It does not humiliate; it gladdens. It is ardent with heart and passion. It is brilliant with imagination. It is fragrant with taste and grace. It is alert, active, and triumphant with splendid mental achievements and practical good deeds. And it is the goodness of a great poet — the poet of natural beauty, of romantic legend, of adventure, of chivalry, of life in its heyday of action and its golden glow of pageantry and pleasure. It found expression, and it wields invincible and immortal power, through an art whereof the charm is the magic of sunrise and sunset, the sombre, holy silence of mountains, the pensive solitude of dusky woods, the pathos of ancient, ivy-mantled ruins, and ocean's solemn, everlasting chant. Great powers have arisen in English literature; but no romance has hushed the voice of the author of *Waverley*, and no harp has drowned the music of the Minstrel of the North.

The publication of a new book by Sir Walter Scott is a literary event of great importance. The time has been when the announcement of such a novelty would have roused the reading public as with the sound of a trumpet. That sensation, familiar in the early part of the present century, is possible no more. Yet there are thousands of persons all over the world through whose hearts the thought of it sends a thrill of joy. The illustrious author of *Marmion* and of *Waverley* passed away in 1832: and now (1890), at the distance of fifty-eight years, his private *Journal* is made a public possession. It is the bestowal of a great privilege and benefit. It is like hearing the voice of a deeply-loved and long-lamented friend suddenly speaking from beyond the grave.

In literary history the position of Scott is unique. A few other authors, indeed, might be named toward whom the general feeling was once exceedingly cordial, but in no other case has the feeling entirely lasted. In the case of Scott it endures in undiminished fervour. There are, of course, persons to whom his works are not interesting and to whom his personality is not significant. Those persons are the votaries of the photograph, who wish to see upon the printed page the same sights that greet their vision in the streets and in the houses to which they are accustomed. But those prosy persons constitute only a single class of the public. People in general are impressible through the romantic instinct that is a part of human nature. To that instinct Scott's writings were addressed, and also to the heart that commonly goes with it. The spirit that responds to his genius is universal and perennial. Caprices of taste will reveal themselves and will vanish; fashions will rise and will fall; but these muta-ions touch nothing that is elemental and they will no more displace Scott than they will displace Shakespeare.

The *Journal* of Sir Walter Scott — valuable for its copious variety of thought, humour, anecdote, and chronicle — is precious, most of all, for the confirmatory light that it casts upon the character of its writer. It has long been known that Scott's nature was exceptionally noble, that his patience was beautiful, that his endurance was heroic. These pages disclose to his votaries that he surpassed even the highest ideal of him that their affectionate partiality has formed. The period that it covers was that of his adversity and decline. He began it on November 20, 1825, in his town house, No. 39 Castle street, Edinburgh, and he continued it, with almost daily entries — except for various sadly significant breaks, after July 1830 — until April 16, 1832. Five months later, on September 21, he was dead. He opened it with the expression of a regret that he had not kept a regular journal during the whole of his life. He had just seen some chapters of Byron's vigorous, breezy, off-hand memoranda, and the perusal of those inspiring pages had revived in his mind the long-cherished, often-deferred plan of keeping a diary. "I have myself lost recollection," he says, "of much that was interesting, and I have deprived my family and the public of some curious information by not carrying this resolution into effect." Having once begun the work he steadily persevered in it, and evidently he found a comfort in its companionship. He wrote directly, and therefore fluently, setting down exactly what was in his mind from day to day; but, as he had a well-stored and well-ordered mind, he wrote with reason and taste, seldom about petty matters, and never in the strain of insipid babble that egotistical scribblers mistake for the spontaneous flow of nature. The facts that he recorded were mostly material facts, and the reflections that he added, whether serious or humorous, were important. Sometimes a bit of history would glide into the current of the chronicle; sometimes a fragment of a ballad; sometimes an analytic sketch of character — subtle, terse, clear, and obviously true; sometimes a memory of the past; sometimes a portraiture of incidents in the present; sometimes a glimpse of political life, a word about painting, a reference to music or the stage, an anecdote, a tale of travel, a trait of social manners, a precept upon conduct, or a thought upon religion and the destiny of mankind. There was no pretence of order and there was no consciousness of an audience; yet the *Journal* unconsciously assumed a symmetrical form; and largely because of the spontaneous operation of its author's fine literary instinct it became a composition worthy of the best readers. It is one of the saddest and one of the strongest books ever written.

The original manuscript of this remarkable work is contained in two volumes, bound in vellum, each volume being furnished with a steel clasp that can be fastened. The covers are slightly tarnished by time. The paper is yellow with age. The handwriting is fine, cramped, and often obscure. "This hand of mine," writes Scott (vol. i. page 386), "gets to be like a kitten's scratch, and will require much deciphering, or, what may be as well for the writer, cannot be deciphered at all. I am sure I cannot read it myself." The first volume is full of writing; the second about half full. Toward the end the record is almost illegible. Scott was then at Rome, on that melancholy, mistaken journey whereby it had been hoped, but hoped in vain, that he would recover his health. The last entry that he made is this unfinished sentence: "We slept reasonably, but on the next morning ——." It is not known that he ever wrote a word after that time. Lockhart, who had access to his papers, made some use of the *Journal* in his *Life of Scott*, which is one of the best biographies in our language ; but the greater part of it was withheld from publication till a more auspicious time for its perfect candour of speech. To hold those volumes and to look upon their pages — so eloquent of the great author's industry, so significant of his character, so expressive of his inmost soul — was almost to touch the hand of the Minstrel himself, to see his smile, and to hear his voice. Now that they have fulfilled their purpose, and imparted their inestimable treasure to the world, they are restored to the ebony cabinet at Abbotsford, there to be treasured among the most precious relics of the past. "It is the saddest house in Scotland," their editor, David Douglas, said to me, when we were walking together upon the Braid Hills, "for to my fancy every stone in it is cemented with tears." Sad or glad, it is a shrine to which reverent pilgrims find their way from every quarter of the earth, and it will be honoured and cherished forever.

The great fame of Scott had been acquired by the time he began to write his *Journal*, and it rested upon a broad foundation of solid achievement. He was fifty-four years old, having been born August 15, 1771, the same year in which Smollett died. He had been an author for about thirty years — his first publication, a translation of Bürger's *Lenore*, having appeared in 1796, the same year that was darkened by the death of Robert Burns. His social eminence also had been established. He had been sheriff of Selkirk for twenty-five years. He had been for twenty years a clerk of the Court of Session. He had been for five years a baronet, having received that rank from King George IV., who always loved and admired him, in 1820. He had been for fourteen years the owner of Abbotsford, which he bought in 1811, occupied in 1812, and completed in 1824. He was yet to write *Woodstock*, the six tales called *The Chronicles of the Canongate*, *The Fair Maid of Perth*, *Anne of Geierstein*, *Count Robert of Paris*, *Castle Dangerous*, the *Life of Napoleon*, and the lovely *Stories from the History of Scotland*. All those works, together with many essays and reviews, were produced by him between 1825 and 1832, while also he was maintaining a considerable correspondence, doing his official duties, writing his *Journal,* and carrying a suddenly imposed load of debt — which finally his herculean labours paid — amounting to £130,000. But between 1805 and 1817 he had written *The Lay of the Last Minstrel, Ballads and Lyrical Pieces, Marmion, The Lady of the Lake, The Vision of Don Roderick, Rokeby, The Lord of the Isles, The Field of Waterloo,* and *Harold the Dauntless,* — thus creating a great and diversified body of poetry, then in a new school and a new style, in which, although he has often been imitated, he never has been equalled. Between 1814 and 1825 he had likewise produced *Waverley, Guy Mannering, The Antiquary, Old Mortality, The Black Dwarf, Rob Roy, The Heart of Midlothian, A Legend of Montrose, The Bride of Lammermoor, Ivanhoe, The Monastery, The Abbot, Kenilworth, The Pirate, the Fortunes of Nigel, Peveril of the Peak, Quentin Durward, St. Ronan's Well, Redgauntlet, The Betrothed,* and *The Talisman.* This vast body of fiction was also a new creation in literature, for the English novel prior to Scott's time was the novel of manners, as chiefly represented by the works of Richardson, Fielding, and Smollett. That admirable author, Miss Jane Porter, had, indeed, written the *Scottish Chiefs* (1809), in which the note of imagination, as applied to the treatment of historical fact and character, rings true and clear; and probably that beautiful book should be remembered as the beginning of English historical romance. Scott himself said that it was the parent, in his mind, of the Waverley Novels. But he surpassed it. Another and perhaps a deeper impulse to the composition of those novels was the consciousness, when Lord Byron, by the publication of *Childe Harold* (the first and second cantos, in 1812), suddenly checked or eclipsed his immediate popularity as a poet, that it would be necessary for him to strike out a new path. He had begun *Waverley* in 1805 and thrown the fragment aside. He took it up again in 1814, wrought upon it for three weeks and finished it, and so began the career of "the Great Unknown." The history of literature presents scarce a comparable example of such splendid industry sustained upon such a high level of endeavour, animated by such a glorious genius, and resultant in such a noble and beneficent fruition. The life of Balzac, whom his example inspired, and who may be accounted the greatest of French writers since Voltaire, is perhaps the only life that drifts suggestively into the scholar's memory as he thinks of the prodigious labours of Sir Walter Scott.

During the days of his prosperity Scott maintained his manor at Abbotsford and his town-house in Edinburgh, and he frequently migrated from one to the other, dispensing a liberal hospitality at both. He was not one of those authors who think that there is nothing in the world but pen and ink. He esteemed living to be more important than writing about it, and the development of the soul to be a grander result than the production of a book. "I hate an author that's all author," said Byron; and in this virtuous sentiment Scott participated. His character and conduct, his unaffected modesty as to his own works, his desire to found a great house and to maintain a stately rank among the land-owners of his country, have, for this reason, been greatly misunderstood by dull people. They never, indeed, would have found the least fault with him if he had not become a bankrupt; for the mouth of

every dunce is stopped by practical success.
When he got into debt, though, it was discovered that he ought to have had a higher
ambition than the wish to maintain a place
among the landed gentry of Scotland; and
even though he ultimately paid his debts —
literally working himself to death to do it —
he was not forgiven by that class of censors;
and to some extent their chatter of paltry
disparagement still survives. While he was
rich, however, his halls were thronged with
fashion, rank, and renown. Edinburgh, still
the stateliest city on which the sun looks
down, must have been, in the last days of
George III., a place of peculiar beauty, opulence, and social brilliancy. Scott, whose
father was a Writer to the Signet, and who
derived his descent from a good old Border
family — the Scotts of Harden — had, from
his youth, been accustomed to refined society
and elegant surroundings. He was born and
reared a gentleman, and a gentleman he
never ceased to be. His father's house was
in George Square (No. 25), then an aristocratic quarter, now somewhat fallen into the
sere and yellow. In that house, as a boy,
he saw some of the most distinguished men
of the age. In after years, when his fortunes were ripe and his fame as a poet had

been established, he drew around himself a kindred class of associates. The record of his life blazes with splendid names. As a lad of fifteen, in 1786, he saw Burns, then twenty-seven, and in the heyday of fame; and he also saw Dugald Stewart, seventeen years his senior. Lord Jeffrey was his contemporary and friend — only two years younger than himself. With Henry Mackenzie, "the Addison of Scotland" — born in the first year of the last Jacobite rebellion, and therefore twenty-six years his senior — he lived on terms of cordial friendship. David Hume, who died when Scott was but five years old, was one of the great celebrities of his early days; and doubtless Scott saw the Calton Hill when it was as Jane Porter remembered it, "a vast green slope, with no other buildings breaking the line of its smooth and magnificent brow but Hume's monument on one part and the astronomical observatory on the other." He knew John Home, the author of *Douglas*, who was his senior by forty-seven years; and among his miscellaneous prose writings there is an effective review of Home's works, which was written for the *Quarterly*, in March 1827. Among the actors his especial friends were John Philip Kemble, Mrs.

Siddons, the elder Mathews, John Bannister, and Daniel Terry. He knew Yates also, and he saw Miss Foote, Fanny Kemble, and the Mathews of our day as "a clever, rather forward lad." Goethe was his correspondent. Byron was his friend and fervent admirer. Wordsworth and Moore were among his visitors and especial favourites. The aged Dr. Adam Ferguson was one of his intimates. Hogg, when in trouble, always sought him, and always was helped and comforted. He was the literary sponsor for Thomas Campbell. He met Madame D'Arblay, who was nineteen years his senior, when she was seventy-eight years old; and the author of *Evelina* talked with him, in the presence of old Samuel Rogers, then sixty-three, about her father, Dr. Burney, and the days of Dr. Johnson. He was honoured with the cordial regard of the great Duke of Wellington, a contemporary, being only two years his senior. He knew Croker, Haydon, Chantrey, Landseer, Sydney Smith, and Theodore Hook. He read *Vivian Grey* as a new publication and saw Disraeli as a beginner. Coleridge he met and marvelled at. Mrs. Coutts, who had been Harriet Mellon, the singer, and who became the Duchess of St.

Albans, was a favourite with him. He knew and liked that savage critic William Gifford. His relations with Sir Humphry Davy, seven years his senior, were those of kindness. He had a great regard for Lord Castlereagh and Lord Melville. He liked Robert Southey, and he cherished a deep affection for the poet Crabbe, who was twenty-three years older than himself, and who died in the same year. Of Sir George Beaumont, the fond friend and wise patron of Wordsworth, who died in February 1827, Scott wrote that he was " by far the most sensible and pleasing man I ever knew." Amid a society such as is indicated by those names Scott passed his life. The brilliant days of the Canongate indeed were gone, when all those wynds and closes that fringe the historic avenue from the Castle to Holyrood were as clean as wax, and when the loveliest ladies of Scotland dwelt amongst them, and were borne in their chairs from one house of festivity to another. But New street, once the home of Lord Kames, still retained some touch of its ancient finery. St. John street, where once lived Lord Monboddo and his beautiful daughter, Miss Burnet (immortalised by Burns), and where (at No. 10) Ballantyne often convoked admirers of the unknown author of *Waverley*, was still a cleanly place. Alison Square, George Square, Buccleuch Place, and kindred quarters were still tenanted by the polished classes of the stately old-time society of Edinburgh. The movement northward had begun but as yet it was inconsiderable. In those old drawing-rooms Scott was an habitual visitor, as also he was in many of the contiguous county manors — in Seton House, and Pinkie House, and Blackford, and Ravelstone, and Craigcrook, and Caroline Park, and wherever else the intellect, beauty, rank, and fashion of the Scottish capital assembled; and it is certain that after his marriage, in December 1797, with Miss Charlotte Margaret Carpenter the scenes of hospitality and of elegant festival were numerous and gay, and were peopled with all that was brightest in the ancient city, beneath his roof-tree in Castle street and his turrets of Abbotsford.

There came a time, however, when the fabric of Scott's fortunes was to be shattered and his imperial genius bowed into the dust. He had long been a business associate with Constable, his publisher, and also with Ballantyne, his printer. The publishing business failed and they were ruined together. It has long been customary to place the blame for that catastrophe on Constable alone. Mr. Douglas, who has edited the *Journal* with characteristic discretion and taste, records his opinion that "the three parties — printer, publisher, and author — were equal sharers in the imprudences that led to the disaster"; and he directs attention to the fact that the charge that Constable ruined Scott was not made during the lifetime of either. It matters little now in what way the ruin was induced. Mismanagement caused it, and not misdeed. There was a blunder, but there was no fraud. The honour of all the men concerned stands vindicated before the world. Moreover, the loss was retrieved and the debt was paid — Scott's share of it in full: the other shares in part. It is to the period of this ordeal that Scott's *Journal* mainly relates. Great though he had been in prosperity, he was to show himself greater amid the storms of disaster and affliction. The earlier pages of the diary are cheerful, vigorous, and confident. The mind of the writer is in no alarm. Presently the sky changes and the tempest breaks; and from that time onward you behold a spectacle of indomitable will, calm resolution, inflexible purpose, patient endurance, steadfast industry, and productive genius that is simply sublime. Many facts of living interest and many gems of subtle thought and happy phrase are found in his daily record. The observations on immortality are in a fine strain. The remarks on music, on dramatic poetry, on the operation of the mental faculties, on painting, and on national characteristics, are freighted with suggestive thought. But the noble presence of the man overshadows even his best words. He lost his fortune in December 1825. His wife died in May 1826. On the pages that immediately follow his note of this bereavement Scott has written occasional words that no one can read unmoved, and that no one who has suffered can read without a pang that is deeper than tears.

But his spirit was slow to break. "Duty to God and to my children," he said, "must teach me patience." Once he speaks of "the loneliness of these watches of the night." Not until his debts were paid and his duties fulfilled would that great soul yield. "I may be bringing on some serious disease," he remarks, "by working thus hard; if I had once justice done to other folks, I do not much care, only I would not like to suffer long pain." A little later the old spirit shows itself: "I do not like to have it thought that there is any way in which I can be beaten. . . . Let us use the time and faculties which God has left us, and trust futurity to His guidance. . . . I want to finish my task, and then good-night. I will never relax my labour in these affairs either for fear of pain or love of life. I will die a free man, if hard working will do it. . . . My spirits are neither low nor high — grave, I think, and quiet — a complete twilight of the mind. . . . God help — but rather God bless — man must help himself. . . . The best is, the long halt will arrive at last and cure all. . . . It is my dogged humour to yield little to external circumstances. . . . I shall never see the threescore and ten, and shall be summed up at a discount. No help for it, and no matter either." In the mood of mingled submission and resolve denoted by these sentences (which occur at long intervals in the story), he wrought at his task until it was finished. By *Woodstock* he earned £8000; by the *Life of Napoleon* £18,000; by other writings still other sums. The details of his toil appear day by day in these simple pages, tragic through all their simplicity. He was a heart-broken man from the hour when his wife died, but he sustained himself by force of will and sense of honour, and he endured and worked till the end without a murmur; and when he had done his task he laid down his pen and died.

The lesson of Scott's *Journal* is the most important lesson that experience can teach. It is taught in two words — honour and duty. Nothing is more obvious, from the nature and environment and the consequent condition of the human race, than the fact that this world is not, and was not intended to be, a place of settled happiness. All human beings have troubles, and as the years pass away those troubles become more numerous, more heavy, and more hard to bear. The ordeal through which humanity is passing is an ordeal of discipline for spiritual development. To live in honour, to labour with steadfast industry, and to endure with cheerful patience is to be victorious. Whatever in literature will illustrate this doctrine, and whatever in human example will commend and enforce it, is of transcendent value; and that value is inherent in the example of Sir Walter Scott.

XXI.

ELEGIAC MEMORIALS.

ONE denotement — among many — of a genial change, a relaxation of the old ecclesiastical austerity long prevalent in Scotland, is perceptible in the lighter character of her modern sepulchral monuments. In the old churchyard of St. Michael, at Dumfries, the burial-place of Burns, there is a hideous, dismal mass of misshapen, weather-beaten masonry, the mere aspect of which — before any of its gruesome inscriptions are read — is a rebuke to hope and an alarm to despair. Thus the religionists of old tried to make death terrible. Much of this same order of abhorrent architecture — the ponderous exponent of immitigable woe — may be found in the old Greyfriars churchyard in Edinburgh, and in that of the Canongate. But the pilgrim to the Dean cemetery and the Warriston — both comparatively modern, and beautifully situated at different points on the north side of the Water of Leith — finds them adorned with every grace that can hallow the repose of the dead, or soothe the grief, or mitigate the fear, or soften the bitter resentment of the living. Hope, and not despair, is the spirit of the new epoch in religion, and it is hope not merely for a sect but for all mankind.

The mere physical loveliness of those cemeteries may well tempt you to explore them; but no one will neglect them who cares for the storied associations of the past. Walking in the Dean, on an afternoon half-cloudy and half-bright, when the large trees that guard its western limit and all the masses of foliage in the dark ravine of the Leith were softly rustling in the balmy summer wind, while overhead and far around the solemn cawing of the rooks mingled sleepily with the twitter of the sparrows, I thought, as I paced the sunlit aisles, that Nature could nowhere show a scene of sweeter peace. In this gentle solitude has been laid to its everlasting rest all that could die of some of the greatest leaders of thought in modern Scotland. It was no common experience to muse beside the tomb of Francis Jeffrey — the formidable Lord Jeffrey of *The Edinburgh Review*.

He lies buried near the **great** wall on the western side of the Dean cemetery, with his wife beside him. A flat, oblong stone tomb, imposed upon a large stone platform and overshadowed with tall trees, marks the place, on one side of which is written that once-famous and dreaded name, now spoken with indifference or not spoken at all: "Francis Jeffrey. Born Oct. 23, 1773. Died Jan. 25, 1850." On the end of the tomb is a medallion portrait of Jeffrey, in **bronze.** It is a profile, and it shows a symmetrical head, a handsome face — severe, refined, frigid — and altogether it is the de**notement of a** personality remarkable for **the faculty** of taste and the instinct of decorum, though not for creative power. Close by Lord Jeffrey, a little to the south, are buried Sir Archibald Alison, the **historian** of Europe, and Henry Cockburn, the great jurist. Combe, the philosopher, rests near the south front of the wall that bisects **this** cemetery from east to west. Not far from the memorials of these famous persons **is** a shaft of honour to Lieutenant John Irving, who was one of the companions of **Sir** John Franklin, and who perished amid the Polar ice in King William's Land in 1848-49.

In another part of the ground a tall cross commemorates David Scott, the painter (1807–1849), presenting a superb effigy of his head, in one of the most animated pieces of bronze that have copied human life. Against the eastern wall, on the terrace overlooking the ravine and the rapid Water of Leith, stands the tombstone of John Blackwood, " Editor of *Blackwood's Magazine* for thirty-three years : Died at Strathtyrum, 29th Oct. 1879. Age 60." This inscription, cut upon a broad white marble, with scroll-work at the base, and set against the wall, is surmounted with a coat of arms, in gray stone, bearing the motto, " Per vias rectas." Many other eminent names may be read in this garden of death ; but most interesting of all, and those that most of all I sought, are the names of Wilson and Aytoun. Those worthies were buried close together, almost in the centre of the cemetery. The grave of the great " Christopher North " is marked by a simple monolith of Aberdeen granite, beneath a tree, and it bears only this inscription : " John Wilson, Professor of Moral Philosophy. Born 18th of May, 1785. Died 3d April, 1854." Far more elaborate is the white marble monument — a square tomb, with carvings of recessed Gothic windows on its sides, supporting a tall cross — erected to the memory of Aytoun and of his wife, who was Wilson's daughter. The inscriptions tell their sufficient story : " Jane Emily Wilson, beloved wife of William Edmondstoune Aytoun. Obiit 15 April, 1859." " Here is laid to rest William Edmondstoune Aytoun, D.C.L., Oxon., Professor of Rhetoric and English Literature in the University of Edinburgh. Sheriff of Orkney and Zetland. Born at Edinburgh, 21st June, 1813. Died at Blackhills, Elgin, 4th August, 1865. ' Waiting for the coming of our Lord Jesus Christ.' 1 Cor. i. 7." So they sleep, the poets, wits, and scholars that were once so bright in genius, so gay in spirit, so splendid in achievement, so vigorous in affluent and brilliant life ! It is the old story, and it teaches the old moral.

Warriston, not more beautiful than Dean, is perhaps more beautiful in situation ; certainly it commands a more beautiful prospect. You will visit Warriston for the sake of Alexander Smith ; for you have not forgotten the *Life Drama*, the *City Poems*, *Edwin of Deira*, *Alfred Hagart's Household*, and *A Summer in Skye*. He lies in the northeast corner of the ground, at the foot of a large Iona cross which is bowered by a chestnut-tree. Above him the green sod is like a carpet of satin. The cross is thickly carved with laurel, thistle, and holly, and it bears upon its front the face of the poet, in bronze, and the harp that betokens his art. It is a bearded face, having small, refined features, a slightly pouted, sensitive mouth, and being indicative more of nervous sensibility than of rugged strength. The inscription gives simply his name and dates: "Alexander Smith, Poet and Essayist. Born at Kilmarnock, 31st December, 1829. Died at Wardie, 5th January, 1867. Erected by some of his personal Friends." Standing by his grave, at the foot of this cross, you can gaze straight away southward to Arthur's Seat, and behold the whole line of imperial Edinburgh at a glance, from the Calton Hill to the Castle. It is such a spot as he would have chosen for his sepulchre — face to face with the city that he so dearly loved. Near him on the east wall appears a large slab of Aberdeen granite, to mark the grave of still another Scottish worthy, "James Ballantine, Poet. Born 11th June, 1808. Died 18th Dec., 1877." And midway along the slope of the northern terrace, a little eastward of the chapel, under a freestone monolith bearing the butterfly that is Nature's symbol of immortality, you will see the grave of "Sir James Young Simpson, Bart., M.D., D.C.L. Born 1811. Died 1870." And if you are weary of thinking about the evanescence of the poets you can reflect that there was no exemption from the common lot even for one of the greatest physical benefactors of the human race.

The oldest and the most venerable and mysterious of the cemeteries of Edinburgh is that of the Greyfriars. Irregular in shape and uneven in surface, it encircles its famous old church, in the haunted neighbourhood of the West Bow, and is itself hemmed in with many buildings. More than four centuries ago this was the garden of the Monastery of the Greyfriars, founded by James I. of Scotland, and thus it gets its name. The monastery disappeared long ago: the garden was turned into a graveyard in the time of Queen Mary Stuart, and by her order. The building, called the Old Church, dates back to 1612, but it was burnt in 1845 and subsequently restored. Here the National Covenant was subscribed (1638) by the lords and by the people, and in this doubly consecrated ground are laid the remains of many of those heroic Covenanters who subsequently suffered death for conscience and their creed. There is a large book of *The Epitaphs and Monumental Inscriptions in Greyfriars Churchyard* made by James Brown, keeper of the grounds, and published in 1867. That record does not pretend to be complete, and yet it mentions no less than two thousand two hundred and seventy-one persons who are sepulchred in this place. Among those sleepers are Duncan Forbes of Culloden; Robert Mylne, who built a part of Holyrood Palace; Sir George Mackenzie, the persecutor of the Covenanters; Carstares, the adviser of King William III.; Sir Adam Ferguson; Henry Mackenzie; Robertson and Tytler, the historians; Sir Walter Scott's father; and several of the relatives of Mrs. Siddons. Captain John Porteous, who was hanged in the Grass-market by riotous citizens of Edinburgh, on the night of September 7, 1736, and whose story is so vividly told in *The Heart of Midlothian*, was buried in the Greyfriars Churchyard, "three dble. pace from the S. corner Chalmers' tomb" (1736). James Brown's record of the churchyard contains various particulars, quoted from the old church register. Of William Robertson, minister of the parish, who died in 1745, we read that he "lies near the tree next Blackwood's ground." "Mr. Allan Ramsay," says the same quaint chronicle, "lies 5 dble. paces southwest the blew stone: A poet: old age: Buried 9th January 1758." Christian Ross, his wife, who preceded the aged bard by fifteen years, lies in the same grave. Sir Walter Scott's father was laid there on April 18, 1799, and his daughter Anne was placed beside him in 1801. In a letter addressed to his brother Thomas, in 1819, Sir Walter wrote: "When poor Jack was buried in the Greyfriars churchyard, where my father and Anne lie, I thought their graves more encroached upon than I liked to witness." The remains of the Regent Morton were, it is said, wrapped in a cloak and secretly buried there at night — June 2, 1581 — low down toward the northern wall. The supposed grave of the superb Latin poet George Buchanan ("the elegant Buchanan," Dr. Johnson calls him) is not distant from this spot; and in the old church may be seen a beautiful window, a triple lancet, in the south aisle, placed there to commemorate that illustrious author.

Hugh Miller and Dr. Chalmers were laid in the Grange cemetery, which is in the southern part of the city, near Morningside. Adam Smith is commemorated by a heavy piece of masonry, over his dust, at the south end of the Canongate churchyard, and Dugald Stewart by a ponderous tomb at the north end of it, where he was buried, as also by the monument on the Calton Hill. It is to see Ferguson's gravestone, however, that the pilgrim explores the Canongate churchyard — and a dreary place it is for the last rest of a poet. Robert Burns placed the stone, and on the back of it is inscribed: "By special grant of the managers to Robert Burns, who erected this stone, this burial-place is to remain for ever sacred to Robert Ferguson." That poet was born September 5, 1751, and died October 16, 1774. These lines, written by Burns, with an intentional reminiscence of Gray, whose *Elegy* he fervently admired, are his epitaph —

" No sculptured marble here, nor pompous lay,
   No storied urn nor animated bust —
This simple stone directs pale Scotia's way
   To pour her sorrows o'er her Poet's dust."

One of the greatest minds of Scotland, and indeed of the world, was David Hume, who could think more clearly and express his thoughts more precisely and cogently upon great subjects than almost any metaphysician of our English-speaking race. His tomb is in the old Calton cemetery, close by the prison, a grim Roman tower, predominant over the Waverley Vale and visible from every part of it. This structure is open to the sky, and within it and close around its interior edge nine melancholy bushes are making a forlorn effort to grow in the stony soil that covers the great historian's dust. There is an urn above the door of this mausoleum and surmounting the urn is this inscription: "David Hume. Born April 26th, 1711. Died August 25th, 1776. Erected in memory of him in 1778." In another part of this ground you may find the sepulchre of Sir Walter Scott's friend and publisher, Archibald Constable, born 24th February 1774, died 21st July 1827. Several priests were roaming over the cemetery when I saw it, making its dismal aspect still more dismal by that rook-like, unctuous, furtive aspect which often marks the ecclesiastic of the Roman Catholic church.

Another great man, Thomas de Quincey, is buried in the old churchyard of the West church, that lies in the valley just beneath

the west front of the crag of Edinburgh
Castle. I went to that spot on a bright
and lovely autumn evening. The place
was deserted, except for the presence of a
gardener, to whom I made my request that
he would guide me to the grave of De Quincey. It is an inconspicuous place, marked
by a simple slab of dark stone, set against
the wall, in an angle of the enclosure, on a
slight acclivity. As you look upward from
this spot you see the grim, magnificent castle frowning on its precipitous height. The
grave was covered thick with grass, and in
a narrow trench of earth cut in the sod
around it many pansies and marigolds were
in bloom. Upon the gravestone is written:
"Sacred to the memory of Thomas de
Quincey, who was born at Greenhay, near
Manchester, August 15th, 1785, and died
in Edinburgh, December 8th, 1859. And
of Margaret, his wife, who died August 7,
1837." Just over the honoured head of the
illustrious sleeper were two white daisies
peeping through the green; one of which I
thought it not a sin to take away — for it is
the symbol at once of peace and hope, and
therefore a sufficient embodiment of the
best that death can teach.

XXII.

SCOTTISH PICTURES.

STRONACHLACHER, LOCH KATRINE, September 1, 1890. — No one needs to be told that the Forth bridge is a wonder. All the world knows it, and knows that the art of the engineer has here achieved its masterpiece. The bridge is not beautiful, whether viewed from afar or close at hand. You see it — or some part of it — from every height to which you mount in Edinburgh. It is visible from the Calton Hill, from the Nelson column, from the Scott monument, from the ramparts of the Castle, from Salisbury Crags, from the Braid Hills, and of course from the eminence of Arthur's Seat. Other objects of interest there are which seek the blissful shade, but the Forth bridge is an object of interest that insists upon being seen. The visitor to the shores of the Forth need not mount any height in order to perceive it, for all along those shores, from Dirleton to Leith and from Elie to Burntisland, it frequently comes into the picture. While, however, it is not beautiful, it impresses the observer with a sense of colossal magnificence. It is a more triumphant structure even than the Eiffel tower, and it predominates over the vision and the imagination by the same audacity of purpose and the same consummate fulfilment which mark that other marvel and establish it in universal admiration. Crossing the bridge early this morning I deeply felt its superb potentiality, and was charmed likewise with its pictorial effect. That effect is no doubt due in part to its accessories. Both ways the broad expanse of the Forth was visible for many miles. It was a still morning, overcast and mournful. There was a light breeze from the southeast, — the air at that elevation being as sweet as new milk. Beneath, far down, the surface of the steel-gray water was wrinkled like the scaly back of a fish. Midway a little island rears its spine of rock out of the stream. Westward at some distance rises a crag, on which is a tiny lighthouse-tower, painted red. The long, graceful stone piers that stretch into the Forth at this point, — which are breakwaters to form a harbour, — and all the little gray houses of Queensferry, Inverkeithing, and the adjacent villages looked like the toy buildings which are the playthings of children. A steamboat was making her way up the river, while near the shores were many small boats swinging at their moorings, for the business of the day was not yet begun. Over this scene the scarce-risen sun, much obscured by dull clouds, cast a faint rosy light — and even while the picture was at its best we glided away from it into the pleasant land of Fife.

In former days the traveller to Stirling commonly went by the way of Linlithgow, which is the place where Mary Stuart was born, and he was all the more prompted to think of that enchanting woman because he usually caught a glimpse of the ruins of Niddry Castle — one of the houses of her faithful Lord Seton — at which she rested, on the romantic and memorable occasion of her flight from Loch Leven. Now, since the Forth bridge has been opened, the most direct route to Stirling is by Dunfermline. And this is a gain, for Dunfermline is one of the most interesting places in Scotland. That Malcolm of whom we catch a glimpse when we see a representation of Shakespeare's tragedy of *Macbeth* had a royal castle there nine hundred years ago, of which a fragment still remains; and on a slope of the coast, a few miles west from Dunfermline, the vigilant antiquarian has fixed the site of Macduff's castle, where Lady Macduff and her children were slaughtered by the tyrant. In the ancient church at Dunfermline, the church of the Holy Trinity, — devastated at the Reformation, but since restored, — you may see the great blue-gray stone which covers the tomb of Malcolm and of Margaret, his queen — an angel among women when she lived, and worthy to be remembered now as the saint that her church has made her. The body of Margaret, who died at Edinburgh Castle, November 16, 1093, was secretly and hastily conveyed to Dunfermline, and there buried, — Edinburgh Castle (The Maiden Castle it was then called) being assailed by her husband's brother, Donald Bane. The remains of that noble and devoted woman, however, do not rest in that tomb, for long afterward, at the Reformation, they were taken away, and after various wanderings were enshrined at the church of St. Lawrence in the Escurial. I had often stood in the little chapel that this good queen founded in Edinburgh Castle, — a place which they desecrate now, by using it as a shop for the sale of pictures and memorial trinkets, — and I was soon to stand in the ruins of Saint Oran's chapel in far Iona, which also was built by her; and so it was with many reverent thoughts of an exalted soul and a beneficent life that I saw the great dark tower of Dunfermline church vanish in the distance. At Stirling the rain, which had long been lowering, came down in floods, and after that for many hours there was genuine Scotch weather and a copious abundance of it. This also is an experience, and, although that superb drive over the mountain from Aberfoyle to Loch Katrine was marred by the wet, I was well pleased to see the Trosach country in storm, which I had before seen in sunshine. It is a land of infinite variety, and lovely even in tempest. The majesty of the rocky heights; the bleak and barren loneliness of the treeless hills; the many thread-like waterfalls which, seen afar off, are like rivulets of silver frozen into stillness on the mountain-sides; the occasional apparition of precipitous peaks, over which presently are driven the white streamers of the mist — all these are striking elements of a scene which blends into the perfection of grace the qualities of gentle beauty and wild romance. Ben

Lomond in the west and Ben Venue and
Ben Ledi in the north were indistinct, and
so was Ben A'an in its nearer cloud; but a
brisk wind had swept the mists from Loch
Drunkie, and under a bleak sky the smooth
surface of "lovely Loch Achray" shone
like a liquid diamond. An occasional grouse
rose from the ferns and quickly winged its
way to cover. A few cows, wet but indifferent, composed, and contented, were now
and then visible, grazing in that desert;
while high upon the crags appeared many
sure-footed sheep, the inevitable inhabitants
of those solitudes. So onward, breathing
the sweet air that here was perfumed by
miles and miles of purple heather, I descended through the dense coppice of birch
and pine that fringes Loch Katrine, and all
in a moment came out upon the levels of the
lake. It was a long sail down Loch Katrine
for a pilgrim drenched and chilled by the
steady fall of a penetrating rain; but Ellen's
Isle and Fitz-James's silver strand brought
pleasant memories of one of the sweetest
of stories, and all the lonesome waters
seemed haunted with a ghostly pageant of
the radiant standards of Roderick Dhu.
To-night the mists are on the mountains,
and upon this little pine-clad promontory of

Stronachlacher the darkness comes down early and seems to close it in from all the world. The waters of Loch Katrine are black and gloomy and no sound is heard but the rush of the rain and the sigh of the pines. It is a night for memory and for thought, and to them let it be devoted.

> The night-wind that sobs in the trees —
> Ah, would that my spirit could tell
> What an infinite meaning it breathes,
> What a sorrow and longing it wakes!

XXIII.

IMPERIAL RUINS.

OBAN, SEPTEMBER 4, 1890. — Going westward from Stronachlacher a drive of several delicious miles, through the country of Rob Roy, ends at Inversnaid and the shore of Loch Lomond. The rain had passed, but under a dusky, lowering sky the dense white mists, driven by a fresh morning wind, were drifting along the heath-clad hills, like a pageant of angels trailing robes of light. Loch Arklet and the little shieling where was born Helen, the wife of the Macgregor, were soon past — a peaceful region smiling in the vale; and presently, along the northern bank of the Arklet, whose copious, dark, and rapid waters, broken into foam upon their rocky bed, make music all the way, I descended that precipitous road to Loch Lomond which, through many a devious turning and sudden peril in the fragrant coppice, reaches safety at last in one of the wildest of Highland glens. This drive is a chief delight of Highland travel, and it appears to be one that "the march of improvement"— meaning the extension of railways — can never abolish; for, besides being solitary and beautiful, the way is difficult. You easily divine what a sanctuary that region must have been to the bandit chieftain, when no road traversed it save perhaps a sheep-track or a path for horses, and when it was darkly covered with the thick pines of the Caledonian forest. Scarce a living creature was anywhere visible. A few hardy sheep, indeed, were grazing on the mountain slopes; a few cattle were here and there couched among the tall ferns; and sometimes a sable company of rooks flitted by, cawing drearily overhead. Once I saw the slow-stepping, black-faced, puissant Highland bull, with his menacing head and his dark air of suspended hostility and inevitable predominance. All the cataracts in those mountain glens were at the flood because of the continuous heavy rains of an uncommonly wet season, and at Inversnaid the magnificent waterfall — twin sister to Lodore and Aira Force — came down in great floods of black and silver, and with a long resounding roar that seemed to shake the forest. Soon the welcome sun began to pierce the mists; patches of soft blue sky became visible through rifts in the gray; and a glorious rainbow, suddenly cast upon a mountain-side of opposite Inveruglas, spanned the whole glittering fairy realm with its great arch of incommunicable splendour. The place of Rob Roy's cavern was seen, as the boat glided down Loch Lomond, — a snug nest in the wooded crag, — and, after all too brief a sail upon those placid ebon waters, I mounted the coach that plies between Ardlui and Crianlarich. Not much time will now elapse before this coach is displaced — for they are building a railroad through Glen Falloch, which, running southerly from Crianlarich, will skirt the western shore of Loch Lomond and reach to Balloch and Helensburgh, and thus will make the railway communication complete, continuous, and direct between Glasgow and Oban. At intervals all along the glen were visible the railway embankments, the piles of "sleepers," the heaps of steel rails, the sheds of the builders, and the red flag of the dynamite blast. The new road will be a popular line of travel. No land "that the eye of heaven visits" is lovelier than this one. But it may perhaps be questioned whether the exquisite loveliness of the Scottish Highlands will not become vulgarised by over-easiness of accessibility. Sequestration is one of the elements of the beautiful, and numbers of people invariably make common everything upon which they swarm. But nothing can debase the unconquerable majesty of those encircling mountains. I saw "the skyish head" of Ben More, at one angle, and of Ben Lui at another, and the lonely slopes of the Grampian hills; and over the surrounding pasture-land, for miles and miles of solitary waste, the thick, ripe heather burnished the earth with brown and purple bloom and filled the air with dewy fragrance.

This day proved capricious, and by the time the railway train from Crianlarich had sped a little way into Glen Lochy the landscape was once more drenched with wild blasts of rain. Loch-an-Beach, always gloomy, seemed black with desolation. Vast mists hung over the mountain-tops and partly hid them; yet down their fern-clad and heather-mantled sides the many snowy rivulets, seeming motionless in the impetuosity of their motion, streamed in countless ribands of silver lace. The mountain ash, which is in perfect bloom in September, bearing great pendent clusters of scarlet berries, gave a frequent touch of brilliant colour to this wild scenery. A numerous herd of little Highland steers, mostly brown and black, swept suddenly into the picture as the express flashed along Glen Lochy, and at beautiful Dalmally the sun again came out with sudden transient gleams of intermittent splendour; so that gray Kilchurn and the jewelled waters of sweet Loch Awe, and even the cold and grim grandeur of the rugged Pass of Brander, were momentarily clothed with tender, golden haze. It was afternoon when I alighted in the seaside haven of Oban; yet soon, beneath the solemn light of the waning day, I once more stood amid the ruins of Dunstaffnage Castle and looked upon one of the most representative, even as it is one of the most picturesque, relics of the feudal times of Scottish history. You have to journey about three miles out of the town in order to reach that place, which is upon a promontory where Loch Etive joins Loch Linnhe. The carriage was driven to it through a shallow water and across some sands which soon a returning tide would deeply submerge. The castle is so placed that, when it was fortified, it must have been well-nigh impregnable. It stands upon a broad, high, massive, precipitous rock, looking seaward toward Lismore island. Nothing of that old fortress now remains except the battlemented walls, upon the top of which there is a walk, and portions of its towers, of which originally there were but three. The roof and the floors are gone. The courtyard is turfed, and over the surface within its enclosure the grass grows thick and green, while weeds and wild-flowers fringe its slowly mouldering walls, upon which indeed several small trees have rooted themselves, in crevices stuffed with earth. One superb ivy-tree, of great age and size, covers much of the venerable ruin, upon its inner surface, with a wild luxuriance of brilliant foliage. There are the usual indications in the masonry, showing how the area of this castle was once subdivided into rooms of various shapes and sizes, some of them large, in which were ample fireplaces and deeply recessed embrasures, and no doubt arched casements opening on the inner court. Here dwelt the early kings of Scotland. Here the national story of Scotland began. Here for a long time was treasured the Stone of Destiny (Lia Fail) before it was taken to Scone Abbey, thence to be borne to London by Edward I., in 1296, and placed, where it has ever since remained, and is visible now, in the old coronation chair in the chapel of Edward the Confessor, at Westminster. Here through the slow-moving centuries many a story of love, ambition, sorrow, and death has had its course and left its record. Here, in the stormy, romantic period that followed 1745, was imprisoned for a while the beautiful, intrepid, constant, and noble Flora Macdonald — who had saved the person and the life of the fugitive Pretender, after the fatal defeat and hideous carnage of Culloden. What pageants, what festivals, what glories and what horrors have those old walls beheld! Their stones seem agonised with ghastly memories and weary with the intolerable burden of hopeless age; and as I stood and pondered amid their gray decrepitude and arid desolation, — while the light grew dim and the evening wind sighed in the ivy and shook the tremulous wall-flowers and the rustling grass, — the ancient, worn-out pile seemed to have a voice and to plead for the merciful death that should put an end to its long, consuming misery and dumb decay. Often before, when standing alone among ruins, have I felt this spirit of supplication, and seen this strange, beseechful look, in the silent, patient stones: never before had it appealed to my heart with such eloquence and such pathos. Truly nature passes through all the experience and all the moods of man, even as man passes through all the experience and all the moods of nature.

On the western side of the courtyard of Dunstaffnage stands a small stone building, accessible by a low flight of steps, which bears upon its front the sculptured date 1725, intertwined with the letters AE. C. and LC., and the words Laus Deo. This was the residence of the ancient family of Dunstaffnage, prior to 1810. From the battlements I had a wonderful view of adjacent lakes and engirdling mountains, — the jewels and their giant guardians of the lonely land of Lorn, — and saw the red sun go down over a great inland sea of purple heather and upon the wide waste of the desolate ocean. These and such as these are the scenes that make this country distinctive, and that have stamped their impress of stately thought and romantic sentiment upon its people. Amid such scenes the Scottish national character has been developed, and under their influence have naturally been created the exquisite poetry, the enchanting music, the noble art and architecture, and the austere civilisation of imperial Scotland.

After dark the rain again came on, and all night long, through light and troubled slumber, I heard it beating on the window-panes. The morning dawned in gloom and drizzle, and there was no prophetic voice to speak a word of cheer. One of the expeditions that may be made from Oban comprehends a visit to Fingal's Cave, on the island of Staffa, and to the ruined cathedral on Saint Columba's island of Iona, and, incidentally, a voyage around the great island of Mull. It is the most beautiful, romantic, diversified, and impressive sail that can be made in these waters. The expeditious itinerant in Scotland waits not upon the weather, and at an early hour this day I was speeding out of Oban, with the course set for Lismore Light and the Sound of Mull.

XXIV.

THE LAND OF MARMION.

BERWICK-UPON-TWEED, September 8, 1890. — It had long been my wish to see something of royal Berwick, and our acquaintance has at length begun. This is a town of sombre gray houses capped with red roofs; of elaborate, old-fashioned, disused fortifications; of dismantled military walls; of noble stone bridges and stalwart piers; of breezy battlement walks, fine sea-views, spacious beaches, castellated remains, steep streets, broad squares, narrow, winding ways, many churches, quiet customs, and ancient memories. The present, indeed, has marred the past in this old town, dissipating the element of romance and putting no adequate substitute in its place. Yet the element of romance is here, for such observers as can look on Berwick through the eyes of the imagination; and even those who can imagine nothing must at least perceive that its aspect is regal.

Viewed, as I had often viewed it, from the great Border bridge between England and Scotland, it rises on its graceful promontory, — bathed in sunshine and darkly bright amid the sparkling silver of the sea, — a veritable ocean queen. To-day I have walked upon its walls, threaded its principal streets, crossed its ancient bridge, explored its suburbs, entered its municipal hall, visited its parish church, and taken long drives through the country that encircles it; and now at midnight, sitting in a lonely chamber of the King's Arms and musing upon the past, I hear not simply the roll of a carriage wheel or the footfall of a late traveller dying away in the distance, but the music with which warriors proclaimed their victories and kings and queens kept festival and state. This has been a pensive day, for in its course I have said farewell to many lovely and beloved scenes. Edinburgh was never more beautiful than when she faded in the yellow mist of this autumnal morning. On Preston battlefield the golden harvest stood in sheaves, and the meadows glimmered green in the soft sunshine, while over them the white clouds drifted and the peaceful rooks made wing in happy indolence and peace. Soon the ruined church of Seton came into view, with its singular stunted tower and its venerable gray walls couched deep in trees, and around it the cultivated, many-coloured fields and the breezy, emerald pastures stretching away to the verge of the sea. A glimpse — and it is gone. But one sweet picture no sooner vanishes than its place is filled with another. Yonder, on the hillside, is the manor-house, with stately battlement and tower, its antique aspect softened by great masses of clinging ivy. Here, nestled in the sunny valley, are the little stone cottages, roofed with red tiles and bright with the adornment of arbutus and hollyhock. All around are harvest-fields and market-gardens, — the abundant dark green of potato-patches being gorgeously lit with the intermingled lustre of millions of wild-flowers, white and gold, over which drift many flights of doves. Sometimes upon the yellow level of the hay-fields a sudden wave of brilliant poppies seems to break, — dashing itself into scarlet foam. Timid, startled sheep scurry away into their pastures as the swift train flashes by them. A woman standing at her cottage door looks at it with curious yet regardless gaze. Farms teeming with plenty are swiftly traversed, their many circular, cone-topped hayricks standing like towers of amber. Tall, smoking chimneys in the factory villages flit by and disappear. Everywhere are signs of industry and thrift, and everywhere also are denotements of the sentiment and taste that are spontaneous in the nature of this people. Tantallon lies in the near distance, and speeding toward ancient Dunbar I dream once more the dreams of boyhood, and can hear the trumpets, and see the pennons, and catch again the silver gleam of the spears of Marmion. Dunbar is left behind, and with it the sad memory of Mary Stuart, infatuated with barbaric Bothwell, and whirled away to shipwreck and ruin, — as so many great natures have been before and will be again, — upon the black reefs of human passion. This heedless train is skirting the hills of Lammermoor now, and speeding through plains of a fertile verdure that is brilliant and beautiful down to the margin of the ocean. Close by Cockburnspath is the long, lonely, melancholy beach that well may have been in Scott's remembrance when he fashioned that weird and tragic close of the most poetical and pathetic of his works, while, near at hand, on its desolate headland, the grim ruin of Fast Castle, — which is deemed the original of his Wolf's Crag, — frowns darkly on the white breakers at its surge-beaten base. Edgar of Ravenswood is no longer an image of fiction, when you look upon that scene of gloomy grandeur and mystery. But do not look upon it too closely nor too long — for of all scenes that are conceived as distinctively weird it may truly be said that they are more impressive in the imagination than in the actual prospect. This coast is full of dark ravines, stretching seaward and thickly shrouded with trees, but in them now and then a glimpse is caught of a snugly sheltered house, overgrown with flowers, securely protected from every blast of storm. The rest is open land, which many dark stone walls partition, and many hawthorn hedges, and many little white roads winding away toward the shore: for this is Scottish seaside pageantry, and the sunlit ocean makes a silver setting for the jewelled landscape, all the way to Berwick.

The profit of walking in the footsteps of the past is that you learn the value of the privilege of life in the present. The men and women of the past had their opportunity and each improved it after his kind. These are the same plains in which Bruce and Wallace fought for the honour and established the supremacy of the kingdom of Scotland. The same sun gilds these plains to-day, the same sweet wind blows over them, and the same sombre, majestic ocean breaks in solemn murmurs on their shore. "Hodie mihi, cras tibi"—as it was written on the altar skulls in the ancient churches. Yesterday belonged to them; to-day belongs to us—and well will it be for us if we improve it. In such an historic town as Berwick the lesson is brought home to a thoughtful mind with convincing force and significance. So much has happened here—and every actor in the great drama is long since dead and gone! Hither came King John, and slaughtered the people as if they were sheep, and burnt the city—himself applying the torch to the house in which he had slept. Hither came Edward I., and mercilessly butchered the inhabitants,—men, women, and children,—violating even the sanctuary of the churches. Here, in his victorious days, Sir William Wallace reigned and prospered; and here, when Menteith's treachery had wrought his ruin, a fragment of his mutilated body was long displayed upon the bridge. Here, in the castle, of which only a few fragments now remain (these being adjacent to the North British railway station), Edward I. caused to be confined in a wooden cage that intrepid Countess of Buchan who had crowned Robert Bruce at Scone. Hither came Edward III., after the battle of Halidon Hill, which lies close by this place, had finally established the English power in Scotland. All the princes that fought in the wars of the Roses have been in Berwick and have wrangled over the possession of it. Richard III. doomed it to isolation. Henry VII. declared it a neutral state. By Elizabeth it was fortified, — in that wise sovereign's resolute and vigorous resistance to the schemes of the Roman Catholic church for the subjugation of her kingdom. John Knox preached here, in a church on Hide Hill, before he went to Edinburgh to shake the throne with his tremendous eloquence. The picturesque, unhappy James IV. went from this place to Ford Castle and Lady Heron, and thence to his death, at Flodden Field. Here it was that Sir John Cope first paused in his fugitive ride from the fatal field of Preston, and here he was greeted as affording the only instance in which the first news of a defeat had been brought by the vanquished general himself. And within sight of Berwick ramparts are those perilous Farne islands, where, at the wreck of the steamer Forfarshire, in 1838, the heroism of a woman wrote upon the historic page of her country, in letters of imperishable glory, the name of Grace Darling. There is a monument to her memory in Bamborough churchyard. Imagination, however, has done for this region what history could never do. Each foot of this ground was known to Sir Walter Scott, and for every lover of that great author each foot of it is hallowed. It is the Border Land, — the land of chivalry and song, — the land that he has endeared to all the world — and you come to it mainly for his sake.

"Day set on Norham's castled steep,
And Tweed's fair river, broad and deep,
And Cheviot's mountains lone."

The village of Norham lies a few miles west of Berwick, upon the south bank of the Tweed, — a group of cottages clustered around a single long street. The buildings are low and are mostly roofed with dark slate or red tiles. Some of them are thatched, and grass and flowers grow wild upon the thatch. At one end of the main highway is a market-cross, near to which is a little inn. Beyond that and nearer to the Tweed, which flows close beside the place, is a church of great antiquity, set toward the western end of a long and ample churchyard, in which many graves are marked with tall, thick, perpendicular slabs, many with dark, oblong tombs, tumbling to ruin, and many with short, stunted monoliths. The church tower is low, square, and of enormous strength. Upon the south side of the chancel are five windows, beautifully arched, — the dog-toothed casements being uncommonly complete specimens of that ancient architectural device. This church has been "restored" — the south aisle in 1846, by I. Bononi; the north aisle in 1852, by E. Gray. The western end of the churchyard is thickly masked in great trees, and looking directly east from this point your gaze falls upon all that is left of the stately Castle of Norham — built by Flamberg of Durham in 1121, and restored by another Prince of that See in 1174. It must once have been a place of tremendous fortitude and of great extent. Now it is wide open to the sky, and nothing of it remains but roofless walls and crumbling arches, on which the grass is growing and the pendent bluebells tremble in the breeze. Looking through the embrasures of the east wall you see the tops of large trees that are rooted in the vast trench below, where once were the dark waters of the moat. All the courtyards are covered now with sod, and quiet sheep nibble and lazy cattle couch where once the royal banners **floated** and plumed and belted knights stood round their king. It was a day of uncommon beauty — golden with sunshine and fresh **with a** perfumed air; and nothing **was** wanting **to** the perfection of solitude. **Near at hand a** thin stream of pale blue **smoke curled** upward from a cottage chimney. At some distance the sweet voices of playing children mingled with the chirp of small birds and **the** occasional cawing of the rook. **The** long grasses that grow upon the ruin moved faintly, **but** made no sound. A few doves **were** seen, gliding in and out of crevices in **the** mouldering turret. And over all, **and** calmly and coldly speaking the survival of nature when the grandest works of man are dust, sounded the rustle of many branches **in** the heedless **wind.**

The day was setting over Norham as I **drove away,** — the red sun slowly obscured in a great **bank of** slate-coloured cloud, — **but** to the last I bent my gaze upon it, and that picture of ruined magnificence can never fade out of my mind. The road eastward toward Berwick is a green lane, running between harvest-fields, which now were thickly piled with golden sheaves, while over them swept great flocks of sable rooks. There are but few trees in that landscape — scattered groups of the ash and the plane — to break the prospect. For a long time the stately ruin remained in view, — its huge bulk and serrated outline, relieved against the red and gold of sunset, taking on the perfect semblance of a colossal cathedral, like that of Iona, with vast square tower, and chancel, and nave: only, because of its jagged lines, it seems in this prospect as if shaken by a convulsion of nature and tottering to its momentary fall. Never was illusion more perfect. Yet as the vision faded I could remember only the illusion that will never fade — the illusion that a magical poetic genius has cast over those crumbling battlements; rebuilding the shattered towers, and pouring through their ancient halls the glowing tide of life and love, of power and pageant, of beauty, light, and song.

THE END.

NOTE.

The POEMS which, under the title *At Vesper Time*, were associated with the foregoing sketches, in previous editions of *Gray Days and Gold*, have been omitted here. They will, however, be included in a new edition, shortly to be published, of *Wanderers* — under which title a collection of the author's principal POEMS has been for some time in circulation.

THE WORKS OF
WILLIAM WINTER.

SHAKESPEARE'S ENGLAND. 18mo, Cloth, 75 Cents.

GRAY DAYS AND GOLD. 18mo, Cloth, 75 Cents.

SHADOWS OF THE STAGE. 18mo, Cloth, 75 Cents.

OLD SHRINES AND IVY. 18mo, Cloth, 75 Cents.

Also a Small Limited Large Paper Edition. 4 Vols. Uniform. $8.00.

WANDERERS: A Collection of Poems. New Edition. With a Portrait. 18mo, Cloth, 75 Cents.

"The supreme need of this age in America is a practical conviction that progress does not consist in material prosperity, but in spiritual advancement. Utility has long been exclusively worshipped. The welfare of the future lies in the worship of beauty. To that worship these pages are devoted, with all that implies of sympathy with the higher instincts, and faith in the divine destiny of the human race."—*From the Preface to Gray Days and Gold.*

MACMILLAN & CO.,

112 Fourth Avenue,   NEW YORK.

(1)

WANDERERS;

BEING

A Collection of the Poems of William Winter.

New Edition, Revised and Enlarged. With a Portrait of the Author.

18MO, CLOTH, 75 CENTS.

Also a Limited LARGE PAPER EDITION, printed on English Hand-made Paper. Price $2.50.

"But it has seemed to the author of these poems — which of course are offered as absolutely impersonal — that they are the expression of various representative moods of human feeling and various representative aspects of human experience, and that therefore they may possibly possess the inherent right to exist." — *From the Preface.*

"The verse of Mr. Winter is dedicated mainly to love and wine, to flowers and birds and dreams, to the hackneyed and never-to-be-exhausted repertory of the old singers. His instincts are strongly conservative; his confessed aim is to belong to 'that old school of English Lyrical Poetry, of which gentleness is the soul, and simplicity the garment.'" — *Saturday Review.*

"The poems have a singular charm in their graceful spontaneity." — *Scots Observer.*

"Free from cant and rant — clear cut as a cameo, pellucid as a mountain brook. It may be derided as trite, *borné*, unimpassioned; but in its own modest sphere it is, to our thinking, extraordinarily successful, and satisfies us far more than the pretentious mouthing which receives the seal of over-hasty approbation." — *Athenæum.*

MACMILLAN & CO.,

112 FOURTH AVENUE,   NEW YORK.

SHADOWS OF THE STAGE.

18mo, Cloth, 75 Cents.

"The fame of the actor more than that of any other artist is an evanescent one — a 'bubble reputation' — indeed, and necessarily so from the conditions under which his genius is exercised. While the impression it makes is often more vivid and inspiring for the moment than that of the poet and the painter, it vanishes almost with the occasion which gave it birth, and lives only as a tradition in the memory of those to whom it had immediately appealed. 'Shadows they are, and shadows they pursue.'

"The writer, therefore, who, gifted with insight and a poetic enthusiasm which enables him to discern on the one hand the beauties in a dramatic work not perceived by the many, and on the other the qualities in the actor which have made him a true interpreter of the poet's thought, at the same time possessing the faculty of revealing to us felicitously the one, and the other is certainly entitled to our grateful recognition.

"Such a writer is Mr. William Winter, easily the first, — for we know of none other living in this country, or in the England he loves so much, in whose nature the critic's vision is united with that of the poet so harmoniously. . . .

"Over and above all this, there is in these writings the same charm of style, poetic glamour and flavor of personality which distinguish whatever comes to us from Mr. Winter's pen, and which make them unique in our literature." — *Home Journal*, New York.

MACMILLAN & CO.,

112 FOURTH AVENUE,   NEW YORK.

OLD SHRINES AND IVY.

18MO, CLOTH, 75 CENTS.

CONTENTS:

SHRINES OF HISTORY.

- I. Storied Southampton.
- II. Pageantry and Relics.
- III. The Shakespeare Church.
- IV. A Stratford Chronicle.
- V. From London to Dover.
- VI. Beauties of France.
- VII. Ely and its Cathedral.
- VIII. From Edinburgh to Inverness.
- IX. The Field of Culloden.
- X. Stormbound Iona.

SHRINES OF LITERATURE.

- XI. The Forest of Arden: As You Like It.
- XII. Fairy Land: A Midsummer Night's Dream.
- XIII. Will o' the Wisp: Love's Labour Lost.
- XIV. Shakespeare's Shrew.
- XV. A Mad World: Anthony and Cleopatra.
- XVI. Sheridan, and the School for Scandal.
- XVII. Farquhar, and the Inconstant.
- XVIII. Longfellow.
- XIX. A Thought on Cooper's Novels.
- XX. A Man of Letters: John R. G. Hassard.

"Whatever William Winter writes is marked by felicity of diction and by refinement of style, as well as by the evidence of culture and wide reading. 'Old Shrines and Ivy' is an excellent example of the charm of his work."—*Boston Courier.*

MACMILLAN & CO.,

112 FOURTH AVENUE,   NEW YORK.

SHAKESPEARE'S ENGLAND.

18MO, CLOTH, 75 CENTS.

"... It was the author's wish, in dwelling thus upon the rural loveliness, and the literary and historical associations of that delightful realm, to afford sympathetic guidance and useful suggestion to other American travellers who, like himself, might be attracted to roam among the shrines of the mother-land. Temperament is the explanation of style; and he has written thus of England because she has filled his mind with beauty and his heart with mingled joy and sadness; and surely some memory of her venerable ruins, her ancient shrines, her rustic glens, her gleaming rivers, and her flower-spangled meadows will mingle with the last thoughts that glimmer through his brain when the shadows of the eternal night are falling and the ramble of life is done." — *From the Preface.*

"He offers something more than guidance to the American traveller. He is a convincing and eloquent interpreter of the august memories and venerable sanctities of the old country." — *Saturday Review.*

"The book is delightful reading." — *Scribner's Monthly.*

"Enthusiastic and yet keenly critical notes and comments on English life and scenery." — *Scotsman.*

MACMILLAN & CO.,

112 FOURTH AVENUE, NEW YORK.

GRAY DAYS AND GOLD.

18MO, CLOTH, 75 CENTS.

CONTENTS.

Classic Shrines.
      Haunted Glens and Houses.
The Haunts of Moore.   Old York.
      Beautiful Bath.
            The Lakes and Fells of Wordsworth.
Shakespeare Relics at Worcester.
      Byron and Hucknall Torkard.
            Historic Nooks and Corners.
Up and Down the Avon.   Shakespeare's Town.
      Rambles in Arden.
            The Stratford Fountain.
                Bosworth Field.
                      The Home of Dr. Johnson.
From London to Edinburgh.
      Into the Highlands.
            Highland Beauties.
                The Heart of Scotland.   Sir Walter Scott.
Elegiac Memorials.
      Scottish Pictures.
            Imperial Ruins.
                The Land of Marmion.
                      At Vesper Time.

This book, which is intended as a companion to *Shakespeare's England*, relates to the gray days of an American wanderer in the British Isles, and to the gold of thought and fancy that can be found there.

MACMILLAN & CO.,

112 FOURTH AVENUE,   NEW YORK.

GRAY DAYS AND GOLD.

18mo, Cloth, 75 Cents.

PRESS NOTICES.

"Mr. Winter's graceful and meditative style in his English sketches has recommended his earlier volume upon (Shakespeare's) England to many readers, who will not need urging to make the acquaintance of this companion book, in which the traveller guides us through the quiet and romantic scenery of the mother-country with a mingled affection and sentiment of which we have had no example since Irving's day."— *The Nation.*

"As friendly and good-humoured a book on English scenes as any American has written since Washington Irving."— *Daily News, London.*

"Much that is bright and best in our literature is brought once more to our dulled memories. Indeed, we know of but few volumes containing so much of observation, kindly comment, philosophy, and artistic weight as this unpretentious little book."— *Chicago Herald.*

"They who have never visited the scenes which Mr. Winter so charmingly describes will be eager to do so in order to realize his fine descriptions of them, and they who have already visited them will be incited by his eloquent recital of their attractions to repeat their former pleasant experiences."— *Public Ledger, Philadelphia.*

MACMILLAN & CO.,

112 Fourth Avenue,   NEW YORK.

IN THE PRESS.

18mo, Cloth, 75 Cents.

SHADOWS OF THE STAGE.

SECOND SERIES.

BY

WILLIAM WINTER.

"Mr. Winter has long been known as the foremost of American dramatic critics, as a writer of very charming verse, and as a master in the lighter veins of English prose." — *Chicago Herald.*

MACMILLAN & CO.,

112 Fourth Avenue,   New York

www.ingramcontent.com/pod-product-compliance
Lightning Source LLC
Chambersburg PA
CBHW031851220426
43663CB00006B/572